Revolution Manifesto

Understanding Marx and Lenin's Theory of Revolution

LIBERATION MEDIA

SAN FRANCISCO

Revolution Manifesto

ISBN: 978-0-9910303-3-0
Library of Congress Control Number: 2015943604

The Bolshevik Revolution: 1917-1923, copyright by E.H. Carr

The State and Revolution by V.I. Lenin is
reprinted from Marxists Internet Archive
Lenin's Collected Works,
Progress Publishers, 1964, Moscow
Volume 25, p. 381-492
www.marxists.org/archive/lenin/works/1917/staterev/.

Editor
Ben Becker

Managing Editor
Eugene Puryear

Staff
Meghann Adams, Jon Britton Anne Gamboni, Paul Greenberg,
Saul Kanowitz, Tina Landis, Mazda Majidi, Susan Muysenberg,
Keith Pavlik, Silvio Rodrigues

Liberation Media
2969 Mission Street #201
San Francisco, CA 94110
(415) 821-6171
books@LiberationMedia.org
www.LiberationMedia.org

Revolution Manifesto

The State and Revolution

Revolution Manifesto

Understanding Marx and Lenin's Theory of Revolution

What is the state?
An overview

BY JANE CUTTER

I N the last year, there has emerged a nationwide movement protesting racist police murders and brutality. The state's coercive power and authority to use violence manifests itself most dramatically in the cold-blooded killing of civilians, including many who were not involved in "criminal activity" when they were killed.

In addition to such deadly incidents, there exists the daily, routine use of coercive force by armed bodies (police forces) throughout the country. New York City's "Stop and Frisk" policy has been replicated under an assortment of names across the country, resulting in the temporary detainment of millions of mainly young Black and Latino people every year. There is also a growing wave of repression that has targeted the activists and organizers who are trying to oppose these injustices.

These are the episodes that have ignited mass anger and protests, but the movement has also called into question the legitimacy of the legal and political system as a whole. To understand and fight state violence and repression, it is imperative to first understand the state.

THE STATE: ARMED BODIES AND COERCIVE INSTITUTIONS

The police are the most obvious symbols of the state or state power. But in conjunction with the police, there are judges who preside over the courts, and prisons and jails that hold more than 2.3 million people in the United States. The police, the courts and the prisons constitute the essence of what Marxists describe as the modern capitalist state.

In addition to the police, courts and prisons, the other primary legal source of organized coercion and violence are the Armed Forces. The U.S. capitalist class rules over not only the working class inside

PHOTO: KEVORK DJANSEZIAN

Police in the United States have become more and more militarized.

this country, but over a vast global network of corporate, financial and commercial interests. The U.S. military consists of more than 2 million people under arms, housed in more than 1,000 military bases and installations around the world.

Although the focus of the military has been to fight foreign wars and maintain military installations and occupation forces in more than 130 countries abroad, the U.S. military has also been dispatched to quell domestic rebellions.

These bodies of armed men and women, the central core of every state, are "special bodies" because they have "special" authority to do what most members of society are not allowed to do: commit violence against other people, detain and imprison them, or launch military actions.

In addition to these bodies, the state also requires a governing superstructure. The form of capitalist government rule varies widely from country to country. During the past three centuries that constitute the era of capitalism, the forms of government have included monarchies, military dictatorships, fascism and democratic republics.

STATE HAS NOT ALWAYS EXISTED

Marxists do not view the state as an eternal institution that has regulated all societies, nor was it made necessary to restrain people from their violent and greedy "human nature." The state is not, as we are often taught, a neutral regulating agency that applies its coercive power equally against all individuals who break the rules or laws of society.

History proves this. There was a long period in human existence when the state did not exist. However, over time, the state emerged in response to particular developments in society that made the state necessary: the emergence of private property and the division of society into classes of "haves" and "have-nots."

Thus, Marxists understand the state to be an organized, coercive power designed to enforce the interests of those individuals who own property as well as the overall system of property ownership in any given era in history. The state is the product of irreconcilable class conflict within a social structure; it seeks to regulate society and this class conflict on behalf of the dominant ruling class.

HOW THE STATE PROTECTS RULING CLASS INTERESTS

When workers go on strike and try to prevent scabs from taking their jobs, the owners can call the police, who will arrest or threaten to arrest the striking workers. The striking workers cannot call police and insist that they arrest the owner.

Landlords can call the police to evict tenants who have not paid the rent. The tenants can lose their homes and be put on the street. Tenants can never call the police and insist that they arrest the landlord because of rent gouging or failure to make repairs. Nor can homeless people simply go and live in empty homes. Why not? Because the police will be called out to defend the banks' rights of property.

Millions of individual working-class people are incarcerated in U.S. prisons. Their crimes usually involve theft or drug use. Contrast their plight to that of the bankers whose fraudulent practices drove the capitalist economy into destruction in 2007. Not one banker was referred for criminal prosecution. Instead, the banks that committed the fraud and criminal wrongdoing were given $700 billion in cash subsidies, and another $6 billion in loan guarantees!

The U.S. state functions to deliver "justice" for the working class while using its vast resources to protect, defend and subsidize the capitalist class.

Revolutionary socialists and communists fight for a revolution that puts poor and working people in power. That will require building an altogether new state to defend the new power and the new system from those who would like to reimpose capitalist exploitation and oppression. Ultimately, with the disappearance of class antagonisms, in a society based on genuine equality where human needs are met, the necessity for special armed bodies (the state as we know it) will disappear. □

Directly from the library to the battlefield

How the ideas of 'The State and Revolution' changed history

BY BRIAN BECKER

ANYONE who aspires to be a real communist or to understand the theory of modern communism must study Lenin's pamphlet "The State and Revolution."

Lenin was able to nearly finish this monumental contribution to Marxism and revolution while on the run, living underground and hiding from the police from August to October 1917, just before the insurrection that seized power.

"The State and Revolution" has been published in practically every written language. It is considered the veritable manifesto for the Russian Revolution. However, the book played no role in the revolution itself given that it was not published until after the workers had seized power in October/November 1917.[1]

The final version was written following the victorious October insurrection. If Lenin had written the book only as a guide to action for the revolution, it would have been unnecessary for him to devote so much time to finishing the book in the two months after the revolution. After all, at this time he and the other leading Bolsheviks were also confronted with the consuming crises and immediate life-and-death challenges facing the new government. The book's primary objective was not simply to serve as a guide to action for the unfolding events. Nor was it to describe what form a future socialist state would take. The book and its contents were written to re-establish the original revolutionary teachings of Marx on the need to smash and destroy the existing state power rather than using its parliamentary apparatus as the path to achieving socialism.

7

The book's primary objective was to rescue Marxism from its devolution into a doctrine of reform, to restore Marxism as a doctrine of revolution.

Lenin writes in "The State and Revolution": "In view of the unprecedentedly widespread distortion of Marxism, our prime task is to re-establish what Marx really taught on the subject of the state."[2]

> *The book's primary objective was to rescue Marxism from its devolution into a doctrine of reform, to restore Marxism as a doctrine of revolution.*

He accuses the leaders of the mass socialist parties of "doctoring" Marxism: "They omit, obliterate and distort the revolutionary side of this teaching, its revolutionary soul. They push to the foreground and extol [in Marx's writing] what is or seems acceptable to the bourgeoisie."

RESTUDYING MARX

The core ideas in "The State and Revolution" were developed by Lenin in January and February of 1917 and were based on his decision to restudy all that Marx and Engels had written on the question of state power.[3] This study took place in a library in Zurich, Switzerland, where Lenin was then in exile.

The core concepts were not developed in response to the prospects, possibilities and challenges of the rapidly unfolding revolutionary process that began in February 1917 and culminated with the Bolshevik-led insurrection in October. Rather, they were developed in response to an ongoing theoretical debate between Karl Kautsky, widely recognized as the leading Marxist theoretician of the international socialist movement, and "left" Marxists.[4]

The question of how the socialists could win political power, and whether the existing state power in capitalist society could be used as an instrument in building socialism, had evolved in a steadily less revolutionary direction since the death of Marx in 1883. Given that the capitalist states had plunged the world into a war of unprecedented destruction, this theoretical dispute was no idle matter but had pressing and immense significance for the general strategy of socialists everywhere.

In this context, Lenin decided to restudy Marx and Engels, and this led him to change or sharpen his own view on the subject.[5]

Although not published until January 1918, the ideas expressed in the book played a fundamental role months earlier in the success of the first socialist seizure of power. Lenin had transmitted the revolutionary essence of these ideas to the Bolshevik leaders, and from there, these ideas guided the party as a whole. Simply put, the October socialist revolution could not have succeeded without the party's leadership, and that leadership would have been impossible had the party not been inculcated with the ideas Lenin developed on the question of the state.

TAKING ON KAUTSKY'S THEORETICAL LEADERSHIP

The book's central ideas represented a sharp departure from the mainstream socialist parties that had become a significant force in Germany and other European parliaments. They also constituted a shift in the thinking of the Bolshevik Party.

"The State and Revolution" was a polemic directed against the core leadership of the parties of the Socialist International (also known as the Second International), and especially against Karl Kautsky and the German Social-Democratic Party, the flagship of international socialism at that time. The mainstream of the socialist movement had forgotten, or chosen to ignore, the conclusions that Marx and Engels developed about the state following the experience of two failed revolutions: the February 1848 revolutions in France and Germany, and, of even greater consequence, the Paris Commune of 1871. In 1871, tens of thousands of Parisian workers were slaughtered and their Commune destroyed following a two-month hold on political power.

Lenin makes clear the primary task of the book in its very first sentences:

What is now happening to Marx's teachings has, in the course of history, happened repeatedly to the teachings of revolutionary thinkers and leaders of oppressed classes struggling for emancipation. During the lifetime of great revolutionaries, the oppressing classes constantly hounded them, received their teachings with the most savage malice, the most furious hatred and the most unscrupulous campaigns of lies and slander. After their death, attempts are made to convert them into harmless icons, to canonize them, so to say, and to surround their *names* with a certain halo for the 'consolation' of the oppressed classes and with the object of duping the latter, while at the same time emasculating the *essence* of the revolutionary teaching, blunting its revolutionary edge and vulgarizing it.[6]

THE EVOLUTION OF MARX AND ENGELS' VIEWS ON REVOLUTION AND THE STATE

Marx and Engels approached political theory as a science. Their theory was based on an examination of facts, evidence, data and experience. They did not engage in much speculation about the future. They did not dream up utopias, schemes or new systems for a better world. Their theory was based on the generalized experience of the class struggle in history.

The "Communist Manifesto" was written on the eve of profound (bourgeois) democratic revolutions that swept France, Germany and other countries in Europe in 1848. Those revolutions ended in violent defeats in 1849 for what Marx and Engels termed the democratic party (representing the peasantry and urban middle classes) and the workers' party (representing the working class). The result was fierce repression of working-class activists for decades to come. Marx and

Barricades during the Paris Commune
where workers seized power for themselves

PHOTO: BRUNO BRAQUEHAIS

Engels were forced to flee Germany and spent the rest of their lives in exile in England.

In France, as a result of an economic crisis that began in England in 1847 and spread to France, a coalition government came to power in February 1848 following the collapse of the regime of King Louis Philippe. The new government promised unemployed workers a job, among other reforms.

In June 1848, the French government moved to close down these economic reforms, and the workers alone defended them against both the big and petty bourgeoisie. Though ending in defeat after a valiant struggle, this was the first time in France that the working class acted politically as an independent force and not as the tail of the radical democratic petty bourgeoisie.

'WINNING THE BATTLE OF DEMOCRACY'

The "Communist Manifesto" had argued that the proletariat must end the political supremacy of the capitalists by attaining or achieving political power, and the state power must be radically altered into the "proletariat organized as the ruling class" and by the working class "winning the battle of democracy."

But the Manifesto had not answered the question of how this task was to be accomplished.

Only the defeats of the revolutions in 1848 allowed Marx to go beyond the Manifesto's general formula and sum up that experience with greater clarity. Studying the 1848 revolutions, he could deal with the question of state power in a specific, particular way, rather than with an abstract formula. In 1852, Marx wrote: "All [earlier] revolutions perfected this machine instead of smashing it."[7] He declared that the proletarian revolution must break up and destroy the state machine.

Marx and Engels considered this conclusion to be an important step forward in their theory of revolution, and foundational to their entire world outlook by 1852.

In an 1852 letter to a follower living in the United States, Marx wrote:

And now as to myself, no credit is due to me for discovering the existence of classes in modern society, nor yet the struggle between them. Long before me bourgeois historians have described the historical development of the struggle of the classes and bourgeois economists the economic anatomy of the classes. What I did that was new was to prove: 1) that the existence of classes is only bound up with particular historical phases in the development of production; 2) that the class struggle necessarily leads to the dictatorship of the proletariat; 3) that the dictatorship itself only constitutes the transition to the abolition of all classes into a classless society.[8]

Marx did not speculate about what form a future workers' state might take. He was not in the business of providing prophesies about what the future "better world" would look like nor what form the "dictatorship of the proletariat" would take. The history of the class struggle had not yet answered that question of what could and would take the place of the smashed and broken up state power.

LEARNING FROM THE PARIS COMMUNE
Only the seizure and holding of political power for two months by the working class in Paris in 1871—the Paris Commune—presented the experience and evidence of what a workers' state would look like and its fundamental difference from the bourgeois state.

The "Communist Manifesto" "has in some details become antiquated," wrote Marx and Engels in 1872,"in view of the practical experience gained, first in the [1848] February Revolution, and then, still more, in the Paris Commune, where the proletariat for the first time held political power for two whole months. ... One thing especially was proved by the Commune, viz., that 'the working class cannot simply lay hold of the ready-made state machinery, and wield it for its own purposes.' "[9]

Marx died 12 years after the Paris Commune. The defeat of the Paris Commune set the movement back, and the First International splintered in its wake. Marx and Engels moved its headquarters from London to New York City, where it contracted further and died a few years later.[10]

There was widespread despair, a mood that accompanies every big setback for the movement. But within a few years a revival began, although in much less revolutionary form. In the decade after Marx's death, Engels functioned as the advisor and consultant to the socialist movements in Europe.[11] As the industrial revolution spread rapidly in the years following the Paris Commune, the workers' struggle changed in form, magnitude and tone. The tempestuous growth of organized labor unions coincided with the expansion of the right to vote. While the Communards in Paris had "stormed the heavens" in raging street fighting, the new socialist movement was channeled into mass union organizing and electoral politics. Socialist parties based in the working class grew exponentially.

Less revolutionary than the Paris Commune but wider in scope, the new socialist parties formed a Second International. Although Marx functioned as an organizational leader of the First International, which did not yet include socialist parties but groups and movements, his ideological and political followers were only a small minority. The Second International by contrast was based on new political parties that possessed a mass base within the working class, and they all identified as Marxists.

Thus the teachings of Marx and Engels became the dominant political force within the Second International. The new international was a huge step forward for Marxism, socialism and the workers' struggle. But as the new workers' parties of the Second International expanded their influence by organizing large trade unions and winning elections in the parliamentary arena, they blunted Marxism's revolutionary essence.

ATTITUDE OF THE GERMAN SOCIAL DEMOCRATIC PARTY AFTER THE DEATH OF MARX

By the early 20th century, the right to vote—for propertyless male workers—had been achieved in large parts of Europe. Mass socialist parties representing the working classes gained ever larger blocs of seats within the parliaments of various countries.

These parties were led by people who considered themselves Marxists and had come to believe that parliamentary struggle was the way to win the "conquest of political power" by the proletariat.

The most important socialist party in Europe was the German Social Democratic Party (SPD). This party and its theoretical leaders, including Karl Kautsky, were considered the "center" of the Socialist

International. Lenin, too, recognized the leadership of the SPD and Kautsky until August 1914, when the SPD delegates in the Reichstag (the German parliament) voted to support the German war effort with the outbreak of WWI.

Kautsky, who was considered by many an orthodox Marxist but actually had become a centrist (revolutionary in words, reformist in deeds), clearly envisioned that the "conquest of political power," as described in the "Communist Manifesto" could be secured through a peaceful, parliamentary path. By gaining the majority in parliament and raising the socialist-led parliament to be the directing force of government, the SPD could chart a path for the socialist reorganization of the economy.

"The goal of our political struggle remains the same as it has been up to now: the conquest of state power through winning a majority in the parliament and raising parliament to be the master of government. Not, however, the destruction of state power," wrote Karl Kautsky in 1912.[12]

For today's reader, it is critically important to understand why this prospect of a peaceful transition to socialism in Germany seemed plausible at the time, rather than just a dream.

Karl Kautsky, major Marxist theoritician, leader of the non-revolutionary wing of German Social Democracy

Germany had anti-socialist laws in place until 1890. Thus, the Social Democratic Party, which had been formed in 1875, had to work under conditions of illegality. When those laws were lifted and the party could function legally, it grew rapidly.

By 1910, the SPD was the most vibrant force in German society. For one, SPD organizers were dominant in the German labor unions. The party published newspapers, magazines, pamphlets and books; it created musical and choir organizations; it established organized networks of worker-poets; it established 125 local children's organizations and 574 youth organizations to provide education, culture and recreational activities for young people; it established a "free advice" program in most cities that provided advice to help working people secure legal and economic benefits from the state; it had its own beer halls where working people gathered.

By 1912, the SPD had grown to nearly a million members. It had in some ways developed a socialist-led "state within the state."[13] SPD leaders and members envisioned an electoral success that would give a mandate for this "state within the state" to be extended nationwide as the new model.

In the 1912 parliamentary elections, the SPD won the largest number of votes of any party, and became the largest bloc within the Reichstag, with 110 seats. Based on this success, the SPD became the "model" for all socialist parties at that time.[14]

But it was precisely because it was so successful as a legal party that its leaders did not want to "lose everything" that they had achieved. When WWI broke out between the competing capitalist governments of Europe, the SPD was forced to decide how its delegates would vote inside parliament. To vote against the expenditures needed for war (war credits) would have had the party labeled as traitors by the German army's high command.

This charge of treason would undoubtedly have also been made by many of the millions of workers who had voted for the SPD. As happens in the beginning of all major wars, a war hysteria swept the population. The threat of annihilation from the "enemy," in this case the reactionary armies of the Russian monarchy, created a wave of patriotism and national unity. To vote against the war funds in this context would have meant standing against this wave and facing the allegation of helping tsarist Russia.

The SPD leadership, along with the other parties in the Socialist International, had seen ahead of time that the danger of a world war was real. In 1912, all the socialist parties had met at a conference in Basel, Switzerland, and vowed that if war came each national party would oppose the workers of their country being sent to kill and be killed by workers from other countries.[15] At the conference, they raised again the banner of the "Communist Manifesto": workers of the world, unite!

On the eve of war, the Manifesto of the Basel Congress called out: "The Congress therefore appeals to you, proletarians and socialists of all countries, to make your voices heard in this decisive hour! Proclaim your will in every form and in all places; raise your protest in the parliaments with all your force; unite in great mass demonstrations. ..."[16]

> 'The Congress therefore appeals to you, proletarians and socialists of all countries, to make your voices heard in this decisive hour!'

But then, in August 1914, the war broke out. With the imperialist powers attacking and invading each other, would the socialists stand aside and oppose their country's armies who were in a life-and-death battle to "save" their nation? To do so certainly meant losing legal status. It meant having mass organizations closed down and their members in parliament sent to prison for treason.

The Russian Social Democratic Labor Party faced the same challenge in August 1914. The Bolshevik faction of the party had won the seats set aside for working-class districts in the parliament (the Duma). Under Lenin's direction, they voted against the war credits.[17] They adhered to the resolution of the Basel Congress. They were imprisoned and indicted as traitors to Russia and went to trial facing the death penalty if convicted.

In Germany, 109 out of the SPD's 110 parliamentary delegates voted for war credits. Karl Liebknecht, a member of the left wing of the SPD, abstained (as had been recommended by Kautsky) but voted "No" on a subsequent resolution. In spite of his parliamentary immunity, Liebknecht was arrested, drafted into the army and dispatched to the Eastern Front of the war against Russia.

THE EVOLUTION IN LENIN'S VIEW OF THE STATE

Lenin's "The State and Revolution" broke with the thinking of the majority of the socialist parties.

Until the outbreak of WWI and the capitulation of the German socialists to the war effort, Lenin had accepted Kautsky as the leading Marxist theoretician of the international movement.

He had not chal-
lenged the dominant
views of other Marx-
ists on the question
of the state. He had
denounced Kautsky as
a traitor to socialism
because of his position
on the war in 1914, but
before 1917 he had not
challenged Kautsky's
view on the state.

*Karl Liebknecht and Rosa Luxembourg,
leaders of the revolutionary wing
of German Social Democracy*

Biographers and
scholars on Lenin
have different views of
whether "The State and
Revolution" was a transformative work that led Lenin to rethink his
own views on the subject.[18] He certainly did not, of course, share
Kautsky's infatuation with the parliamentary road to socialism. Lenin,
for instance, had supported the launching of an armed struggle during
the 1905 Russian Revolution.

But prior to 1917, Lenin did not enter the theoretical debate
between Kautsky and "left-wing" Marxists on the role of the state and
how the socialists could achieve political power.

In 1916, Dutch Marxist Anton Pannekoek and later Russian
Nicholai Bukharin published "leftist" criticisms of Kautsky's position
on the state.

Pannekoek argued that the socialist movement and the cause of
the working class "is not simply a struggle with the bourgeoisie over
state power as an object, but a struggle against state power."[19]

Kautsky responded, as quoted earlier, that a socialist-led government could and should become "the master of government," but
with the aim of using, and not destroying, the state power.

In a 1916 article, Bukharin argued along the same lines as Pannekoek that a new socialist society led by an empowered working
class must "outgrow the framework of the state and burst it from
within as they organize their own state power" or else the new

socialist power would eventually be absorbed by the capitalist state structures. Lenin rejected the article for publication.

Lenin decided to directly participate in the debate between Kautsky and the "left" Marxists in December 1916. His remarks at that point suggest that he considered Kautsky's views closer to the position of orthodox Marxism than Bukharin's:

> Socialists are in favor of using the present state and its institutions in the struggle for the emancipation of the working class, maintaining also that the state should be used for a specific form of transition from capitalism to socialism. This transitional form is the dictatorship of the proletariat, which is *also* a state. The anarchists want to 'abolish' the state, 'blow it up' as Comrade Nota-Bena (Bukharin) expresses it one place, erroneously ascribing this view to the socialists.[20]

In a review of this debate, political scientist Marian Sawer has argued that Lenin's three months devoted to the restudying of Marx and Engels' position on the state was what led to a dramatic change in his own position on the state. As a consequence, she says, Lenin came closer to Bukharin's orientation but then went far beyond anything written by the "left" Marxists in developing a comprehensive position on the need to smash the bourgeois state and replace it with a state of a new type: the commune state.

For the first time, Lenin writes of the worker and peasant soviets (popular councils), which had been created spontaneously from below during the 1905 revolution, as the embryo of a new alternative state power to the capitalist state.

The timing of Lenin's theoretical study on the Marxist view of revolution coincided accidentally with the outbreak of a real revolution. All of the freshly thought-through ideas about the need to smash the state and create a new state power immediately became applicable in life.

With the outbreak of the revolution, all of Lenin's attention switched to finding a way back to Russia without being murdered or jailed along the way. Lenin feared that his notes on Marx and Engels' writings on the state—what became famously known as the Blue

Notebook—could be confiscated on the trip back from Zurich. The notebook was left behind and he was only able to retrieve it later through Sweden. But even without the notes in hand, Lenin was crystal clear on the task at hand.

Even before securing safe passage back to Russia from exile, he wrote: "Thus the St. Petersburg workers, having overthrown the tsarist monarchy, immediately set up their *own* organization, the Soviet of Workers' Deputies, immediately proceeded to strengthen and extend it, to organize independent Soviets of Workers and Soldiers' Deputies. Only a few days after the revolution, the St. Petersburg Soviet of Workers and Soldiers' Deputies comprised over 1,500 deputies of workers and peasants dressed in soldier's uniforms. It enjoyed such wide confidence among railway workers and the entire mass of the laboring population that it began to develop into a real *people's government.*"[22]

CHANGING THE BOLSHEVIK ORIENTATION

Lenin arrived in Russia on April 3, 1917. When he first presented his worked-out thoughts on the state and its practical implications, they sent a shock wave through both the Bolshevik and Menshevik leaderships. Lenin read his "April Theses" out loud to a gathering of Bolshevik leaders on April 4. In fact, he did so twice so that the

The Petrograd Soviet

PHOTO: EVERETT HISTORICAL

meaning of his proposals could be fully understood. The next day, he read them to a meeting of both Bolshevik and Menshevik leaders.

The April Theses represented a major reorientation. Lenin called for the overthrow of the newly created "Provisional" capitalist coalition government that had arisen after the February Revolution and the replacement of this existing state power with a new state power led by grassroots Workers' and Peasants' Councils (Soviets). He invoked the Paris Commune in the April Theses, although without much explanation, and insisted that the comrades reread what Marx wrote about the Commune in 1871, 1872 and 1875.[23]

Both the moderate, Menshevik faction of the Social Democratic Labor Party of Russia and the revolutionary faction of the Bolsheviks rejected Lenin's position. Upon hearing his April Theses at their meeting, the St. Petersburg Committee voted 13-2 to reject the position Lenin offered. The Bolshevik Committee in Moscow also voted to reject the Theses.

Almost all the other Bolshevik leaders were supporting, although in a critical way, the Provisional coalition government that had replaced the fallen tsar in the February Revolution (1917). That new government was dominated by the bourgeois-liberal Cadet Party, the peasant-based Socialist Revolutionaries and the Mensheviks. The Bolsheviks were offering critical support while attempting to push it to the left.

The April Theses and the struggle it provoked inside the Bolshevik Party has been examined and re-examined by socialists and scholars of the Russian Revolution and in all the biographies on Lenin.

THE CLASS CHARACTER OF THE REVOLUTION

Most of these discussions center on just one side of an internal controversy that had been debated for more than a decade but was brought into sharper focus by the April Theses: the class character of the coming revolution.

This was the question of whether the upcoming revolution in Russia, which all sides agreed would fundamentally be a bourgeois-democratic revolution, would be led by the liberal bourgeoisie (the Menshevik position) or by the "democratic dictatorship" of the workers and the peasantry as a whole (the position put forward by Lenin in 1905 and adopted by the Bolsheviks).

According to this formula, Lenin foresaw an alliance between, on the one side, the peasantry including the kulaks (capitalist farmers), middle and small-holding peasants and the landless poor that would neutralize the big bourgeoisie and, on the other side, the working class through the Russian Social Democratic Labor Party, which could play the leading role politically since it would see the way forward that no peasant party possibly could.

Most of the Bolshevik leaders, therefore, believed that Marxists could enter a revolutionary government together with the democratic petty bourgeoisie, even if the workers' party did not rule outright. Rather, the workers' party would play the role of ensuring the best political conditions—a democratic republic—for capitalist development to replace feudalism, and for the workers' struggle against the capitalists.

> *[Lenin] anticipated a bourgeois-democratic revolution but without the bourgeoisie or its political parties leading the fight.*

The implication of Lenin's formula of a "democratic dictatorship" was that the bourgeoisie in Russia was too enfeebled, too tied to the feudal landowners and imperialism, and too unrevolutionary to carry out radical land reform and other measures enacted by the bourgeois revolutions in Europe a century or more earlier. In other words, Lenin's formula of the "democratic dictatorship of the workers and peasantry" anticipated a bourgeois-democratic revolution but without the bourgeoisie or its political parties leading the fight.

When Lenin insisted in April 1917 that the Bolsheviks withdraw support for the Provisional government and instead call for all power to the Soviets, some Bolsheviks argued that Lenin had abandoned his own theory about the bourgeois-democratic stage of the Russian Revolution. They asked how it could be that Russia, if it first required a bourgeois-democratic revolution (against feudalism and its remnants), later followed by a socialist revolution, would only need a bourgeois-democratic revolution as a historical stage that lasted two months?

Lenin would not have considered the April Theses conclusions to be an abandonment of the earlier formula regarding the democratic dictatorship of the workers and peasantry.

He had written two years earlier (October 1915) that this democratic dictatorship would closely connect the bourgeois-democratic revolution and the socialist revolution. "The task confronting the proletariat in Russia is the consummation of the bourgeois-democratic revolution in Russia *in order* to kindle the socialist revolution in Europe."[24]

The second point in the Theses stated: "The specific feature of the present situation in Russia is that the country is *passing* from the first stage of the revolution—which, owing to the insufficient class-consciousness and organization of the proletariat, placed power in the hands of the bourgeoisie—to its second stage, which must place power in the hands of the proletariat and the poorest sections of the peasants."[25]

> 'The task confronting the proletariat in Russia is the consummation of the bourgeois-democratic revolution in Russia in order to kindle the socialist revolution in Europe.'

The Theses' seventh point called for: "The immediate union of all banks in the country into a single national bank, and the institution of control over it by the Soviet of Workers' Deputies." This "transitional demand" suggests that Lenin believed at that point in the revolution that the country, in spite of its economic and social/cultural backwardness, could move in the direction of socialism—though not necessarily to socialism itself. Many bourgeois-democratic revolutions in economically backward countries have carried out nationalizations of banks and major industries to advance the development of capitalism, not socialism.

In the eighth point, Lenin makes this clear: "It is not our *immediate* task to 'introduce' socialism, but only to bring social production and the distribution of products at once under the *control* of the Soviets of Workers' Deputies." (Lenin's emphasis). In light of the horrific destruction and social agony of WWI and its potentially revolutionary consequences not just in Russia but in the advanced capitalist countries as well, Lenin was at this point leaving somewhat open the actual near-term course of the Russian revolution.

But Lenin had already come to the conclusion that the second revolution that he was now advocating as an imminent, short-term prospect—not as an event for the distant future—would be the inauguration of the international socialist revolution. This was so even though Russia was still devoid of the material prerequisites to finish the construction of socialism.

His nuanced views on this were succinctly explained in his "Farewell Letter to the Swiss Workers," written on March 26, just eight days before he returned to Russia and read his April Theses to his startled comrades:

> However, it was not our impatience, nor our wishes, but the *objective conditions* created by the imperialist war that brought the *whole of* humanity to an impasse, that placed it in a dilemma: either allow the destruction of more millions of lives and utterly ruin European civilisation, or hand over power in *all* the civilised countries to the revolutionary proletariat, carry through the socialist revolution.
>
> To the Russian proletariat has fallen the great honour of beginning the series of revolutions which the imperialist war has made an objective inevitability. But the idea that the

V. I. Lenin

PHOTO: UNIVERSALIMAGESGROUP

Russian proletariat is the chosen revolutionary proletariat among the workers of the world is absolutely alien to us. We know perfectly well that the proletariat of Russia is less organised, less prepared and less class-conscious than the proletariat of other countries. It is not its special qualities, but rather the special conjuncture of historical circumstances that *for a certain, perhaps very short,* time has made the proletariat of Russia the vanguard of the revolutionary proletariat of the whole world.

Russia is a peasant country, one of the most backward of European countries. Socialism *cannot* triumph there *directly* and *immediately.* But the peasant character of the country, the vast reserve of land in the hands of the nobility, *may,* to judge from the experience of 1905, give tremendous sweep to the bourgeois-democratic revolution in Russia and *may* make our revolution the prologue to the world socialist revolution, a *step* toward it. ...

In Russia, socialism cannot triumph directly and immediately. But the peasant mass *can* bring the inevitable and matured agrarian upheaval to the point of *confiscating* all the immense holdings of the nobility. ...

Such a revolution would not, in itself, be socialism. But it would give a great impetus to the world labour movement. It would immensely strengthen the position of the socialist proletariat in Russia and its influence on the agricultural labourers and the poorest peasants. It would enable the city proletariat to develop, on the strength of this influence, such revolutionary organisations as the Soviets of Workers' Deputies to replace the old instruments of oppression employed by bourgeois states, the army, the police, the bureaucracy; to carry out—under pressure of the unbearably burdensome imperialist war and its consequences—a series of revolutionary measures to *control* the production and distribution of goods.

Single-handed, the Russian proletariat cannot bring the socialist revolution to a *victorious conclusion*. But it can give the Russian revolution a mighty sweep that would create the most favourable conditions for a socialist revolution, and would, in a sense, start it. It can facilitate the rise of a situation in which its *chief*, its most trustworthy and most reliable collaborator, the *European* and American *socialist* proletariat, could join the decisive battles. (Lenin's emphasis)

SMASHING AND REPLACING THE EXISTING STATE

Lenin's strategic reorientation of the Party and the controversy it created inside the Bolsheviks has been the subject of widespread attention and examination.

But the other side to the April Theses debate has been given less attention. Lenin's thinking had evolved and had now gone much further than others in the socialist and Marxist movement in his insistence on the need to smash, break up the state and replace it with a new one—a power such as that created by the short-lived Paris Commune.

By raising the Soviets as an alternative state power, a new historical iteration of the commune state, Lenin was arguing that these spontaneously created and democratically elected councils of workers', soldiers' and peasants' deputies could not only defend the people's interests and the struggle for democracy but also could function as a new state power. Instead of utilizing the existing state power for socialist ends, the existing state could be broken up, smashed and replaced with a new state based on another class power.

In the 1905 revolution, where soviets had first appeared as a grassroots innovation, Lenin had portrayed the soviets as a kind of united front rather than an embryonic new state power: "The Soviet of Workers' Deputies is not a labor parliament and an organ of self-government at all, but a fighting organization for the achievement of definite aims."

The core argument of the "April Theses" was more ambitious: Lenin was, in effect, proposing the smashing of the existing state and creating an entirely new and fundamentally different type of state.

In Lenin's notebook from the restudy of Marx and Engels' works, it is clear that he re-evaluated the role of the Soviets as the basis for a Commune-type state along the lines of what was created in Paris in 1871 and which Marx analyzed with great detail. That process of examining the experience of the commune had, as stated above, also sharpened Marx's own view on the question of the state and revolution.[26]

> Lenin was, in effect, proposing the smashing of the existing state and creating an entirely new and fundamentally different type of state.

This theoretical study not only sharpened Lenin's views. They were literally brought by him from the library to the battlefield of the revolution itself.

Lenin did not favor calling for the immediate overthrow of the Provisional government by the Soviets. Because the majority of workers and poor peasants were still following and supporting the bourgeois-led Provisional revolutionary government:

We must explain to the masses that the Soviet of Workers Deputies is the only possible form of revolutionary government; and that, therefore, our task is, while this [Soviet] government is submitting to the influence of the bourgeoisie, a patient, systematic and persistent explanation to the masses the error of their tactics.[27]

Lenin believed that the unwillingness of the Provisional government to end Russia's involvement in WWl would lead the workers, based on their own living experience, to come over to the Bolsheviks' attitude about the need for a revolutionary insurrection.

Lenin's authority within the organization and his unmatched respect allowed him to win over the majority of his opponents within a few days. The Bolsheviks reoriented and were on the path to revolution, which they accomplished seven months later.

Lenin's presentation of the "April Theses" was followed by numerous articles, letters and speeches by him during the subsequent months of revolution, setback, repression, renewal and finally the seizure of power. The themes and ideas from April were repeated and re-explained as the tide of events took sharp and unexpected turns.

Beginning in July 1917, after the Mensheviks and Socialist Revolutionaries—who had the majority of delegates in the Soviet—had insisted on continuing the war and had refused to respond to the demands of the peasants for land, the Bolsheviks even temporarily withdrew for a time their call for all power to the Soviets.

This was to avoid the potential misperception among the increasingly restive and radicalized workers that the Bolsheviks call for Soviet power could be interpreted as support for the continuation of the war or that they would turn their backs on the poor peasants who were bent on seizing the lands of the nobility and large landlords.

As the bourgeois-led Provisional government caved to the pressure of Britain, France and the United States to continue the war, the moderate socialists who joined the Provisional government lost credibility among the workers. By September, the tactic of "persistent and patient" explanation about the inadequacies of the Provisional government showed its correctness as public opinion shifted dramatically to the left and the Bolshevik delegates became the elected majority of the Soviets.

Once they had majority support in the Soviets, Lenin insisted that preparations for an insurrection begin. On October 25 (November 7), the Bolshevik-led insurrection brought the Soviets to power. Their political support had become so widespread that the revolution was nearly bloodless.

Lenin emerged from hiding on the day of victory. He spoke briefly to the Meeting of the Petrograd Soviet of Workers' and Soldiers' Deputies and offered a resolution. These brief remarks summarize with complete clarity Lenin's theses on the character of the state and the revolution which created it:

> What is the significance of the workers' and peasants' revolution? Its significance is, first of all, that we shall have a Soviet government, our own organ of power, in which the bourgeoisie will have no share whatsoever. The oppressed masses will themselves create a power. The old state apparatus will be shattered to its foundations and a new administrative apparatus set up in the form of Soviet organizations.[28]

Was the new Soviet power, the new workers' and peasants' government, to be a socialist or a bourgeois-democratic regime? Lenin was as clear as day. The two stages of revolution had become intertwined as a consequence of the international situation. "From now on, a new phase in the history of Russia begins, and this, the third Russian Revolution, should in the end lead to the victory of socialism." He announced the trajectory: "We possess the strength of mass organization, which will overcome everything and lead the proletariat to the world revolution." He ended: "We must now set about building a proletarian socialist state in Russia. Long live the world socialist revolution!"

Lenin's concepts and views on the question of the state and revolution were finally presented in their fullness with the publication of "The State and Revolution" two months later.

SUMMARY

Because its topic is not limited to Russia but to the tasks facing all modern revolutions that seek to overturn power in bourgeois society, and because Lenin and the Bolsheviks actually succeeded in making the revolution in 1917, "The State and Revolution" was embraced in the early 1920s by the international communist movement as a guiding document for the revolutionary struggles of the working class.

Left-wing socialists and pro-communist anarchists united and formed new communist parties to challenge the reformist socialist parties. They were inspired by the Russian Revolution, and "The State and Revolution" became their new manifesto of the 20th century.

But just as Marx and Engels' writings on the state were "forgotten" by the Marxist leaders of the socialist parties and just as these founders of scientific socialism were "converted into harmless icons" and the essence of their revolutionary teachings blunted and vulgarized, so too were the works of Lenin by many of the Marxists who came later.

This was a complicated historical process and went through various stages stretching over several decades. First the victories of Nazism and fascism in Germany, Italy and Spain—and then the spread of fascism throughout continental Europe—not only crushed both the communist and socialist parties but caused a re-orientation away from proletarian revolution in Europe.

Instead of smashing the state and making revolution, most of the communist movement in Europe retreated in its strategy and objectives. The main goal in the short term was to "preserve democracy" and prevent the capture of state power by fascist organizations. Preserving democracy, they thought, meant allying with the liberal bourgeoisie to preserve rather than smash the existing state.

> *The PSL anticipates that the current global contradictions emanating from imperialism and the repeated economic crises of capitalism will lead to a new wave of revolutionary mobilization.*

Assigning this non-revolutionary task to the communist movement required a "reinterpretation" of Lenin's key writings. Since these parties declared themselves to be Marxist-Leninists, it required them, to reinterpret the meaning of Marx and Lenin's foundational texts or ignore their applicability. They had to essentially pretend that they did not exist or have relevance in the modern world. This was precisely how the Second International reformist socialists had vulgarized Marx's view of the state.

The PSL anticipates that the current global contradictions emanating from imperialism and the repeated economic crises of capitalism will lead to a new wave of revolutionary mobilization and the revival of socialism as the only counterpoint to capitalism. That is why we are republishing and restudying "The State and Revolution."

Each new generation of working-class activists and fighters needs to read and study this manifesto of revolution, which restored the essence of Marx's prescription about how to build a better world. ☐

Living and cooperating without a state: studying pre-class society

BY KARINA GARCIA

LENIN defined the state not as the political leadership in a given society but as the organization of force and violence—armies, police, jails, courts—used by one class to repress others. The particular form that a government takes, be it an elected parliament or a military dictatorship, has significance for the form that the class struggle may take in that society.

But regardless of the form of government, which can go through many changes and alterations, the state always defends a particular class in society. Only a social revolution changes which class holds the reins of power.

Under capitalism, a change of faces, administrations or parties does not change the system of exploitation and oppression of the poor and working class.

But do we not need the state?

Frederick Engels put this question into a world-historical context. In his 1884 book, "The Origins of the Family, Private Property and the State," he describes the evolution of human society as a product of social relations, productive capacities and technological advancement. In particular, the gradual division of society into classes—with a tiny exploiting ruling class on top—required the creation of a repressive apparatus to maintain and enforce the ruling class' power and privileges against the lower working classes. These organs of repression were used in the interests of the most powerful or economically dominant class to suppress any revolt or rebellion by the exploited or oppressed

classes. Herein lies the thesis that the state is fundamentally an instrument of repression of one class by another.

Democratic forms have existed in other forms of class rule as
well, not just capitalism. In ancient Greece, for example, citizens partic-
ipated in the decision-making process directly, as opposed to indirectly
through representatives, congresspeople or senators. There were 90,000
Athenian citizens who were eligible to take part in this direct democracy—although there were 365,000 slaves, not to mention the entire
population of women, who were barred from the political process.[1]

The Roman Republic experienced similar types of exclusions,
demonstrating that democracy in these class societies really only
existed for the elites.

Has there been a democratic state without class rule?

Strictly speaking, no. If democracy is a form of class rule, then
a democratic state, as a particular form of repression of one class by
another, would have no reason for existence without classes.

That does not mean that some characteristics popularly associated with democracy—participation of all in society or equality
for all—have not existed in societies before classes. In fact, Engels
devoted substantial attention to studying pre-class societies in order
to show how a society could be organized without oppression.

Engels collected evidence of a social order based on cooperation
and satisfying human needs. Far from the idealistic and unscientific
claims that humanity is inherently good or inherently evil, Engels
showed that human beings are a product of the social and economic
system in which they live.

SOCIETIES WITH NO CLASSES

Engels highlighted the work of American Lewis Henry Morgan.
Morgan's research on ancient societies was the first to show a well-de-
fined social order in cultures with "primitive" economies.

Morgan had emphasized kinship groups, which he described
using the Latin word "gens," as a type of social organization that
bound people together by a common ancestry—typically the female
line of ancestry. This has been generally confirmed by subsequent
anthropological research. Modern anthropologist Richard Lee, for
instance, concluded that the "archeological, historical and ethno-

The !Kung People of Southwestern Africa are the source of
significant knowledge regarding living in pre-class societies.

graphic record" made entirely clear the existence of "autonomous,
non-exploitative human social arrangements."[2]

Indeed, for roughly 100,000 years, human beings lived in these
sorts of "band societies" as they are known in modern anthropology.
One study of the Paleolithic era in the Mediterranean noted that the
bands' focus on hunting large game reflected that "hominid popula-
tions were consistently very small and dispersed" up until roughly
40,000 to 50,000 years ago.[3]

Comprising groups of several dozen, band societies operated on
principles of equality: "There was no differential access to resources
through private land ownership and no specialisation of labour
beyond that of sex. ... The basic principle of egalitarian band societies
was that people made decisions about the activities for which they
were responsible."[4]

Speaking of the !Kung people in Southwest Africa ("!K" in the
name "Kung" is pronounced with a click), Richard Lee noted:

> The !Kung are a fiercely egalitarian people, and
> they have evolved a series of important cultural practices
> to maintain this equality, first by cutting down to size
> the arrogant and boastful, and second by helping those
> down on their luck to get back in the game. ... Men are
> encouraged to hunt as well as they can, but the correct
> demeanour for the successful hunter is modesty and
> understatement.[5]

The study of the Mediterranean cited earlier goes on to note
that "cooperation among hunters ... must have been essential for the
capture of large game animals."[6]

Engels' theoretical presentation was based on the up-to-date
anthropological research of his era. Subsequent research has revised
certain propositions—for instance, that these bands of humans
generally operated in conditions of deprivation. While by present
standards these societies would be considered quite "scarce" in
their material offerings, many were not teetering on conditions of
hunger or extinction, and some enjoyed an abundance of big game
for lengthy periods of time.[7]

In fact, it was likely the expansion of nomadic hunter-gathering
societies across the globe that caused a collapse in the population of
these big-game animals, undermined the communal way of life and
ultimately helped lay the basis for the "Neolithic revolution"—the rise
of settled agriculture.

These early societies were, as Engels and Morgan often noted,
matrilineal—something confirmed recently by an edited volume put
together by the Royal Anthropological Institute.[8] A range of new
genetic studies of hunter-gatherer societies in Africa show that many
were also matrilocal—in which families lived with the family of the
mother, suggesting a tendency towards matrilineality.[9]

From a sexual perspective, these matrilineal clans organized
themselves into broad groups of "brothers" and "sisters." This is a
difficult concept to address in brief, but such institutions and arrangements—which Henry Morgan referred to as "group marriage"—were
upheld by long-standing public opinion and tradition, not by a separate state organization.[10]

Lionel Sims explained in Radical Anthropology:

The women—sisters, mothers and daughters—stay together. The mothers have sons and these sons are brothers to all the women. This is a matrilineal system, in which there are just two family groups: the women in one group have husbands in the other group, and these men's sisters are in turn another group of women. A woman will therefore always have brothers and they will always support her in her dealings with other men from the other clan. They will never let her down, since this is the basis for the clan's existence.

> *'In our culture you lose your brother when he gets married. Our system of families divides us all up. But in a matrilineal clan that never happens.'*

In our culture you lose your brother when he gets married. Our system of families divides us all up. But in a matrilineal clan that never happens. Your first identity is with your brothers and your sisters, and your common line of mothers, who all live in a group. Men as husbands move between the two groups, visiting the women of the other group before returning to their own long house when the seclusion ritual starts and temporary marriage is dissolved.

Imagine the man visiting his wife in the other clan and standing alongside her are all her sisters, all her mothers and all her brothers. You will be under pressure from all of them. So the matrilineal clan is a non-sexual union of economically and politically participating blood kin, and it works through enormously high levels of solidarity.[11]

Stephen Beckerman and Paul Valentine further found that across wide-swaths of low-land South America a system known as "partible paternity" prevailed, in which the responsibility for a woman's offspring fell to multiple men.[12]

Not surprisingly, in such societies, the status of women was enormous and very different from the present. One early European visitor to Iroquois territory noted: "Nothing ... is more real than this superiority of the women ... it is in them that all real authority resides."[13] Engels, however, working from Morgan, assumed a more or less universal matrilineal set of societies in the period of "primitive" communism.

The level of equality between men and women, and the social practices through which it was maintained, are a matter of some dispute among modern anthropologists, who have the benefit of further research.

While there are significant particularities and differences in social and sexual relations across many different societies, this form of family, emphasizing the community over the individual or two-person marriage, can be considered the norm during the Paleolithic period.

In the broad outlines, the basic Marxist argument that societies without classes existed and that they were mostly matrilineal with equality for women is a matter of fact, not debate.

DECISION-MAKING IN PRE-CLASS SOCIETY

Engels emphasized important discoveries in Morgan's research on the gens in the Iroquois Confederacy. He found that not only did key democratic forms such as participation and equality exist in the Iroquois gens but, in addition, they existed without the same contradictions found in class society.

There was no such thing as slavery, inequality or poverty in these societies. All men and women could participate in the collective decisions of the tribe. Leaders were elected by the gens to represent them in federal and tribal council meetings. But their powers were very limited. They possessed no powers of coercion, only a moral authority. They could be immediately recalled by the people.

The concepts of authority and leadership were transformed under class systems such as capitalism, in which "special laws are enacted proclaiming the sanctity and immunity of the officials." In the modern state, Engels said "'The shabbiest police servant' has more 'authority' than the representatives of the clan"—in other words, the power to unilaterally carry out violence against others. But on the other side, even the most powerful military generals under capitalism would never enjoy the "uncoerced respect" that the leaders of the clan earned in pre-class societies.

In pre-class society, there was a division of labor between men and women. Men hunted for food, gathered raw materials and fought in war. Women took care of the home, prepared food and made clothing. Each took possession of their respective tools, but everything else was communal, including housework. The division of sexes did not imply a dominant or unequal relationship between men and women. Each dominated their respective field, and neither received more or less for their work in relation to their needs.

The division of sexes did not imply a dominant or unequal relationship between men and women. Each dominated their respective field, and neither received more or less for their work in relation to their needs.

As a member of a gens, one was obligated to help, protect and especially assist in avenging injury by strangers to another member of the gens. This was a protection that was guaranteed to everyone. But there was no obligation to fight in wars. There were no police, no judges, no prisons, no lawsuits. And yet, as Engels points out, "everything took an orderly course." Weapons were not restricted to this or that special institution like a police or an army distinct from the whole gens.

Quarrels and disputes were settled by the whole community affected. Only as an extreme and exceptional measure was blood revenge threatened. Even then, a process of mediation was sought first, and if that could not console the aggrieved parties, the wronged gens would appoint one or more avengers whose duty it was to pursue and kill the slayer.

All the above goes to show that capitalism, class society and the existence of a state—as special bodies of violence and "authority" standing above society—are not simply a reflection of "human nature." In fact, the vast majority of human experience points to the opposite conclusion. Another world is indeed possible for the simple fact that other worlds have existed in the past.

GOING FORWARD

Morgan was fond of pointing out the liberty, equality and solidarity of these pre-class communities. But he, along with Marx and Engels, understood that this epoch of human development could not be a goal for modern society, "good old days" to try and recapture. Marx and Engels referred to this epoch as "primitive communism," because although the society was organized around cooperation and meeting human needs, it was characterized by "primitive" technologies and productive capacities.

Engels believed that capitalism was approaching a stage where the existence of classes not only would cease to be a necessity for the development of production but become a "positive hindrance" to production. The capitalist class, a class of parasites and leeches, would no longer be necessary for the development of production. Its order, like the order of the gens, was therefore doomed to become outdated and fall.

"The state inevitably falls with [social classes]," Engels wrote. "The society which organizes production anew on the basis of free and equal association of the producers will put the whole state machinery where it will then belong—into the museum of antiquities, next to the spinning wheel and the bronze ax."

Based on these observations, along with the study of class societies and their contradictions, Marx and Engels were able to show the potential for a society without classes or exploitation. The new communism and its collective solidarity would be based on abundance instead of scarcity, planning instead of the joint struggle for survival.

Lenin summarized their position in "State and Revolution":

> Only in communist society, when the resistance of the capitalists has been completely crushed, when the capitalists have disappeared, when there are no classes (i.e. when there is no distinction between the members of society as regards their relation to the social means of production), only then 'the state … ceases to exist,' and 'it becomes possible to speak of freedom.' Only then will a truly complete democracy become possible and be realized, a democracy without any exceptions whatever. And only then will democracy begin to wither away, owing to

the simple fact that, freed from capitalist slavery, from the untold horrors, savagery, absurdities and infamies of capitalist exploitation, people gradually become accustomed to observing the elementary rules of social intercourse that have been known for centuries and repeated for thousands of years in all copybook maxims.[14]

When workers overturn capitalism and its attendant evils—imperialist wars and foreign occupations, overproduction crises, hoarding and the destruction of our natural resources, enforced poverty, a chaotic and unregulated global economy and all of the other crimes of capitalism—then and only then will working people have laid the social foundation and opened the door for the eventual triumph of freedom, equality and solidarity between peoples. □

The U.S. state and the U.S. revolution

BY EUGENE PURYEAR

IT is no exaggeration to say that the principal disputes between activists, organizations and political trends in U.S. social movements have hinged on different understandings of, and attitudes toward, the state.

What distinguishes a revolutionary communist perspective from a reformist perspective is not one of momentary tactics, which may range from the most tempered and patient to the most militant and bold depending on the circumstances. Nor are communists the only people who envision a world without exploitation, oppression and war.

Communists are distinguished fundamentally by how they answer the following question: To build such a new society, can the working class simply lay hold of the ready-made state machinery, or must the working class dismantle the old state and build another one anew?

This is not an abstract theoretical question. It informs all political activity. While reformists of various stripes conduct their organizing to rebuild popular confidence in the existing state, revolutionary communists seek to de-legitimize and expose it. Instead of struggling in the present with an eye towards a new stage of peace with the system, communists struggle now with an eye towards the next, higher stage of struggle against it.

There is clear evidence that the state machinery of the United States cannot be turned into a tool for liberation. Even a limited study of its historical development shows that it must be completely scrapped and replaced.

ORIGINS OF THE U.S. STATE

The state arose as a political form in tandem with class antagonism. At its core are the "special bodies of armed men," institutions that have the special right to use and threaten force to protect the interests of a given society's ruling class.

State institutions are presented as merely "upholding the law." However, the essential function of the state, including the legal system and its laws, is to defend, expand and stabilize that society's property relations. Apart from socialism, under which the working class uses state power to abolish class distinctions altogether, the state has served numerically small property-owning ruling classes that have controlled a disproportionate share of their society's surplus wealth.

States across space and time have many similarities corresponding with their stage of social development. This was a key part of Marx and Engels' concept of historical materialism, as they identified the stages through which very different societies pass (communal, ancient slavery, tributary/feudal, capitalist, socialist and communist).

But to truly understand a state requires going beyond these general labels. A society's particular variation of class exploitation and its history of struggle between and among social classes must be examined.

Those who constructed the U.S. state largely viewed the American continent as a "blank slate." Native nations had built diverse governance and state structures throughout. But those societies were built around entirely different social systems, and were largely of a pre-class character, and thus of little utility for the capitalist and slave-owning ruling classes that settled here.

The United States stands as one of the earliest capitalist states, the third place to undergo a bourgeois revolution (bringing the bourgeoisie to political power).[1] However, unlike the two bourgeois revolutions that preceded it or its European followers, this country's capitalist foundations did not directly emerge from a feudal cocoon.

The "Founding Fathers" were free to set up their state without the need for vestiges of formal aristocratic privilege. They were free to establish a governmental structure centered fundamentally on capital accumulation. This meant two things at the time of the American Revolution: "preparing the ground," so to speak, by expelling and eroding the power of Native nations; and solidifying the rights in property of the leading classes, in particular the planters whose slaves powered the economy.

These two factors loomed large in the creation of the nation-state and speak to why this country's bourgeois revolution essentially had two acts: the American Revolution and the Civil War, in which the unresolved contradictions of 1787 were resolved in 1865.

The Constitution itself is a marker of the unmistakable class character of the state. The Constitution is held up as a semi-sacred document in U.S. schoolrooms and in the ideology of U.S. patriotism as the world's "longest surviving constitution" (ratified in 1789) and therefore proof of the country's "exceptionalism." But its long survival actually proves the Marxist position: that the state institutions, forms of government and social rights of the country descend, without fundamental alteration, from a document that was written by 100 bourgeois and slave-owning white men over two centuries ago. This is not proof of the Constitution's superiority, but rather of the durability of bourgeois rule in the United States, and the Constitution's ongoing utility to the ruling class in defending that rule.

> *The Constitution itself is a marker of the unmistakable class character of the state.*

What follows is a brief sketch of these formative elements of the U.S. state and Constitution, with the intent of further elucidating their class functions, and the need for their replacement.

CAPITALISM, COLONIALISM AND SLAVERY

The colonial settlers who arrived in British North America sought gold in particular and profit in general. Gold was not in the cards in either Virginia or the Massachusetts Bay, Britain's first North American colonies, but once Virginia settler John Rolfe introduced a new strain of stimulant, tobacco (a drug), a solution was found. In addition to timber and others of less importance, the new "cash crop" provided the kindling for an explosion of plantation agriculture.

The opening up of the "new world" offered significant opportunities to exploit the area's resources, to sell goods in the rising market economy in Europe, and to take advantage of the new opportunities for expanded markets in the colonial world itself.

In the five years leading up to the revolution, 63 percent of all exports from mainland British America came from the South-

ILLUSTRATION: MICHAEL HAMPSHIRE

The Hohokam people of what is now the U.S. Southwest constructed a series of canals that lasted over 1,000 years and are still considered an engineering marvel today.

ern colonies, and the vast majority of these exports were from the "cash crops" of tobacco, rice and indigo (cotton came a bit later, after 1776).[2] Dr. W.E.B. Du Bois highlighted the "immense economic advantages" of this "triangular trade," which pivoted on slave labor, to the New England merchant colonies as well.[3]

The colonials viewed themselves mostly as Englishmen and as subjects of the British crown, not as members of a separate nation—at first. A range of issues outside the scope of this article drove the colonies together and into rebellion. The long-term foundation for independence was the shared territory and increased economic interconnectedness of the colonies as a viable political unit with homegrown ruling classes. But the immediate ruptures included: 1) the Crown's desire to keep the expansion of the colonies within clear limits, given that expansion made them less governable and provoked costly wars against Native nations; 2) the English monopoly on colonial trade was clearly restricting the economic potential of the colonies; and 3) the general high-handedness of the King and Parliament as regards colonial affairs, which fueled a cycle of distrust and escalation.[4]

Once independent, the colonial ruling classes did not seek a social revolution that would overturn social and property relations. After all, they already held power. Rather, they constructed a state to entrench the existing social order and remove potential barriers to its expansion.

'LIFE, LIBERTY AND PROPERTY'

In the immediate aftermath of the American Revolution, those leading the process of government formation represented a decisive section of the colonial elite seeking security in property, freedom of commerce and an elite-dominated republic.

For instance, George Washington was the richest man in America. Benjamin Franklin was quite wealthy. Robert Morris, delegate to the Constitutional Convention, was the most significant financier in the soon-to-be United States. William Blount, signer of the Declaration of Independence and North Carolina delegate to the Constitutional Convention, owned a million acres of land. George Mason of Virginia owned tens of thousands of acres of land and 300 slaves.[5]

It is no wonder that for such men the phrase "life, liberty and property" defined the core values of the new state. The "pursuit of happiness" was only substituted for "property" at the last moment because of its better rhetorical flair, but in truth these Founders saw the two phrases as synonymous.

James Madison fretted that the "increase of population will of necessity increase the proportion of those who will labour under all the hardships of life [and] secretly sigh for a more equal distribution of its blessings." If they obtained equal democratic rights, the propertyless might obtain enough numerical clout to take hold of power and institute policies to strip the rich of their property.

His proposal was to greatly restrict the democratic aspects of the new government structure. This included restricting the rights of the propertyless to only vote for one branch of the legislature (the House), to impose high property qualifications for holding office, and to disperse power widely among the states so as to more easily contain future dissension from below.

In the famous Federalist Paper 10, Madison explained that the republican structure of the government is best suited to control factions, "the most common and durable source of [which] has been the various and unequal distribution of property. Those who hold, and those who are without property have ever formed distinct interests in society."

PAINTING: JOHN TRUMBULL

*George Washington, richest man in the colonies, whose
wealth flowed from owning hundreds of slaves*

Madison goes on to state that there is no cure for this, as the division between the rich and the poor is eternal. But the role of the government and its state institutions would be to protect those with the bulk of the property. This was the explicit bias in developing a republican form of government.

The popular vote was kept to a bare minimum, first with a range of property requirements instituted. Even as the property terms were gradually eliminated, Black people and women were totally excluded. Popular elections were only made available for the House of Representatives; U.S. Senators were selected by the leading politicians of each state, while the president was selected by the Electoral College.

Constructing a legal system that protected private property was equally important. John Adams wrote, "The moment the idea is admitted into society that property is not as sacred as the laws of God, and that there is not a force of law and public justice to protect it, anarchy and tyranny commence."

Indeed, Adams' values proved to be long-standing. Despite the protests of modern-day libertarians, the "sacredness" of private property remains the cornerstone of the country's legal code. Making any revisions to the Constitution is difficult and any which would encroach on the rights of the rich—for instance, by creating new social rights to housing, education, health care, or a living income—are practically impossible.

ARMED FORCES AND 'INDIAN REMOVAL'

From the very earliest days, pushing back the Native nations was key to the strategy of the settlers. The colonial settlers desired land and resources, but someone else was living there. Individual truces and treaties notwithstanding—these were moments of peace as prelude to war—the policy of the colonists and later state-builders was extermination and expulsion of the "savages."

The availability of cheap, plentiful and resource-rich land was no small matter. It provided a huge stimulant for the large landowners looking to grow crops and timber, and became a primary avenue for social mobility for the lower classes who came to the continent to escape the ironclad class stratification and misery of the Old World. In this founding period, Native people represented a shared obstacle for the settler classes, and thus the basis for cross-class unity among whites. The ideological counterpart for this cross-class alliance was white supremacy. A key part of Benjamin Franklin's "Albany Plan" was to strengthen the colonies as a unitary political formation that could provide for its own defense—against Native Americans.

The American "army" for most of its existence—up to about the Spanish-American War—was a relatively small land force, growing out of and continually augmented by ad-hoc state-controlled militias, whose principal task was "Indian removal" and "defense" against Native people resisting land encroachments.

The First American Regiment, the first standing armed force of the U.S. government, was established to control the frontier. The larger and more significant Legion of the United States was formed after a crushing defeat of U.S. forces at the hands of the Western Confederacy of Native tribes in the Battle of Wabash. A series of "Militia Acts" followed, which established the ability of the president to call out state militias to coordinate actions against Native nations, and ostensibly "foreign invasion."[6]

For the U.S. generals who directed wars throughout the 20th century, their reference points and heroes were in the wars against Native peoples a century earlier.

Essentially, the birth and development of the U.S. Army is deeply connected to the expansion of the national territory. When these colonial-imperial state forces were later directed to overseas expansion, this was often seen as a projection of the same mission. For the U.S. generals who directed wars throughout the 20th century, their reference points and heroes were in the wars against Native peoples a century earlier.

An echo of this history still resonates loudly in the naming of U.S. military weaponry. As the U.S. empire spreads its deadly forces across the globes, it carries the names, in its helicopters, drones and missiles of the Native peoples it long ago suppressed. Its helicopters are called Apache, Comanche, Chinook, Lakota, Cheyenne and Kiowa—as well as "Black Hawk" (Native warrior). Its destructive missiles are "Tomahawks" and its drones are "Gray Eagles," while Osama Bin Laden was codenamed "Geronimo" for the U.S. special forces pursuing him.

A LEGAL CODE FOR SLAVERY, A VOCABULARY FOR RACISM

In his investigation of the development of white supremacy, communist historian Theodore Allen related:

"During my own study of page after page of Virginia county records, reel after reel of microfilm prepared by the Virginia Colonial Records Project, and other seventeenth-century sources, I have found no instance of the official use of the word "white" as a token of social status before its appearance in a Virginia law passed in 1691, referring to 'English or other white women.'"[7]

Allen's point, of course, is that the ideology of white supremacy emerged not because of timeless antagonisms based on phenotype differences, but in a precise historical context related to the development of racial slavery.

Slavery, in general, has a long and ancient history, operating in a variety of contexts. In general, this history was not ethnocentric. Even in the "Western world," the attitude of the slave societies of classic antiquity towards the "Black world" was, in its inclusiveness, the "extreme reverse" of the 20th century's racist realities (to quote the late Howard University historian Chancellor Williams).[8]

In the early North American colonial period, the labor pool of the developing new economy was based on various forms of servitude but short of outright slavery, such as indenture. At this time, an indentured servant, typically from Europe, was often less costly than a slave.

As the volume of trade grew, changing dynamics in Europe made Africans the more economical and readily available source of labor starting as early as 1640. Moreover, the increased life expectancy of white laborers (beyond the terms of their indenture) threatened to upset the colonies' class balance of forces and the land expansion patterns desired by the ruling classes. Not coincidentally, around the same period a juridical and social effort was made to separate the whites from the Blacks, and to strip the latter of their rights as citizens in general.[9]

In the 17th century, the status of Blacks in the upper south was far from settled, as evidenced by the scope of Black landownership and Black standing in the courts.[10] Toward the end of the century, however, these rights were stripped away. Interracial marriages were banned and, in the words of historian Gary Nash, "In rapid succession slaves lost their right to testify before court, to engage in any kind of commercial activity ... to hold property ... to travel without permission."[11]

Similar processes played out across the Southern colonies, where many planters brought the racist ideology of the West Indies to the mainland as they fled the restive islands in search of "safer" territory for their slaving project.[12]

These and other restrictions were organized to contain the restiveness of the colonies, which included significant cross-racial class solidarity. As is reflected by historian Edmund Morgan's famous quote in his "American Slavery, American Freedom": "it was common, for example, for servants and slaves to run away together, steal hogs together, get drunk together. It was not uncommon for them to make love together."[13]

The potential disruptive nature of this collaboration was amplified for the colonial elite after Bacon's Rebellion, in which multi-racial lower-class discontent resulted in Jamestown being burned down and the governor forced to flee.

The subordination of Black people as a people—or if you prefer a "race"—coincided with the rise of plantation slavery. An elaborate legal and political system, in tandem with new social codes of conduct, "normalized" racial stratification in all aspects of society. This system, protected by state and extra-state violence provided stability to a system that at its bottom was powered by the labor of several million enslaved people.

This carried over into the new nation-state even as the "Founding Fathers" proclaimed their democratic and republican principles, supposedly based on equal rights and citizenship. The enslavement of and denial of rights for Black people was not merely an expression of hypocrisy. Rather, white supremacy provided the foundation for the "democratic republic."

Only having "solved" the question of how to subordinate society's lowest social class—through enslavement—could the ruling class entertain ideas of "political equality" for the rest of society. Likewise, as the new state based its legitimacy on democratic principles, it in turn required a more complete theoretical system to explain the glaring inconsistency.

In most historical slave societies, where ingrained and hereditary class systems already existed, and ruling-class legitimacy rested on explicit and brute force, there had been no need to develop racial theories to justify enslavement. But because the U.S. bourgeoisie had developed a new "democratic shell" to legitimate its power and state, proclaiming a formal end to permanent class divisions, it in fact accelerated the proliferation of racist ideas.

THE EMERGENCE OF U.S. PRISONS AND POLICE FORCES

The police and the prisons in the United States are linked directly to the unique development of U.S. capitalism and the needs of the ruling class in different periods. Capitalism is distinguished from feudal and slave systems in that it rests on a "free labor" market, where the poor and working classes are in competition with one another to "freely" sell their labor power to the highest bidder. But its dynamic and uncontrolled development also produces constant fluctuation, depression and dislocation of the lower classes. In that context, it became necessary for the rulers to create special and sophisticated institutions to deal with the consequences and preserve "order." As explained in "Shackled and Chained," another publication by this author:

> The importation of African slaves expanded through the 1700s and rapidly became the dominant class of unfree labor in the colonial labor market. But indentured servitude and convict labor did not fully disappear until the period following the American Revolution, when the newly independent states in the north gradually abolished slavery and made "free labor"—that is, wage labor—the norm. It is during this period of early capitalist consolidation that the modern prison formed.

> Since the early United States emerged with two distinct but interlinked social systems, capitalism in the north and chattel slavery in the south, it should come as no surprise that the early development of incarceration came with sharp regional distinctions. The most common image that comes to mind of prisons—of specially guarded facilities and prisoners confined to individual cells—originated primarily in the capitalist North. ...

> The U.S. South took a different course from the North. While early on there were some moves to establish northern-style prisons in the South, the pre-Civil War prison system was relatively underdeveloped. With the vast majority of African Americans enslaved, the ability to punish and discipline was left largely to their slaveholders, not the government. Incarcerating a slave, after all, would deprive his master of his labor, and was thus reserved for extraordinary circumstances. ...

The closer the South moved towards a "free" labor market after the abolition of slavery, the more the form of Southern prisons conformed to what was common in the North. These emerged as part of an attempt to re-subjugate Black labor. There is, therefore, a significant link between the two regions' penal systems: the development of modern prisons took place, in a rough sense, as classes of official bound labor were replaced by "free" wage labor. Capitalist development is deeply entangled with the roots of the mass incarceration system.[14]

The same conclusion can be drawn for the modern police, which were also institutionally developed in England and the northern United States in the period of rapid capitalist expansion from the early to mid-1800s. Centrally organized police forces emerged largely out of the failed attempts of the very rich to pacify demonstrations and labor strikes through their private security personnel and brute force alone.

Centrally organized police forces emerged largely out of the failed attempts of the very rich to pacify demonstrations and labor strikes through their private security personnel and brute force alone.

The wealthy worried that without such an additional layer of armed forces to protect their property and "the law," the crowds would quickly overwhelm them.

In the South, police forces emerged largely out of the slave patrols that traveled the countryside to intimidate and brutalize slaves who threatened to challenge the existing order or run away. In Southern cities, where slaves occupied many core jobs but also could have greater opportunities to organize together, police forces were similarly developed and expanded to keep them in line.

Over time, the police took on additional functions and activity, including patrolling, which became a projection of consistent state power and intimidation in communities that were considered sites of unrest.

In neither the case of the prisons nor the police was their emergence due to "rising crime." It was about social control. It took several generations and a lot of propaganda to inoculate the population with the belief that the police were a neutral force protecting "law and order" in the abstract. In nationally oppressed communities, of course, where generations of passed-down experiences show otherwise, that lie is often met with instinctive opposition.

THE BEST POSSIBLE SHELL FOR CAPITALIST EXPLOITATION

Given that the U.S. state developed along the lines of defending the rich, destroying Native peoples and justifying racist enslavement, how has it lasted? If it is so clearly built on injustice and inequality, why has it not been tossed aside by the tens and hundreds of millions of people and "swept into the dustbins of history?"

Russian revolutionary V.I. Lenin remarked in "State and Revolution":

A democratic republic is the best possible political shell for capitalism, and, therefore, once capital has gained possession of this very best shell ... it establishes its power so securely, so firmly, that no change of persons, institutions or parties in the bourgeois-democratic republic can shake it.[15]

In short, for all its enduring features, the U.S. capitalist state has displayed a remarkable malleability. The ruling class has been able to bend and amend it, generation after generation, not only to physically defend its exploitative system but also to absorb many forms of resistance to it.[16]

This has in fact become a hallmark of patriotic lore. Alluding to the rebellion in Ferguson, Missouri, Barack Obama recently cited the ability of the country's political system to handle various insurgencies of nationally oppressed Black people. For Obama, this is proof of America's ability to "solve" its problems, its alleged self-reforming nature.

But the continued erosion of living standards of working people, not to mention all the violence, discrimination and exploitation pervading daily life, shows the limits of this "self-reforming character." That is, after all, why the Black Lives Matter and low-wage worker movements have erupted.

For all the reforms that the system has offered, the basic state institutions and structures defending private property have remained and grown stronger. For the ruling class, every concession to the people's movements has been an effort to re-legitimize its own rule. This flexibility in the form of its rule has fortified the resilience of the U.S. imperialist ruling class.

Determined and heroic struggle has struck down many methods of social control and subjugation: slavery and other forms of unfree labor, Jim Crow segregation, openly discriminatory laws and so on. But the capitalist class has been able to continuously adjust because it is loyal only to its own expansion—not any single form of rule or any single ruling faction.

At the end of the day, the capitalist ruling class retains a military that is devoted to the Empire. It retains an immense police force devoted to preserving "social peace" through intimidation and violence at home. It retains a legal and prison system that is used to target radicals and lock up whole layers of the population whose interests and needs the system cannot address. It retains a Constitution, which—far from being a neutral document—has its deepest roots in the needs and interests of an expanding capital, privileging property over people and expressly designed to limit the ability of the vast majority of people—mostly poor and working class—to influence government. It retains a legislature, which can only be effectively accessed by the wealthy and their friends, that allows the various and competing factions of the ruling class to put forward their respective proposals while measuring their respective strength. It retains an executive branch with immense power that serves to protect the common interests of the bourgeoisie abroad and at home, and to discipline any sector of society that could destabilize that power.

THE OLD STATE MACHINERY MUST BE UPROOTED

All this speaks to the question from the beginning of this article, the key and fundamental truth that Marx expressed in 1871: "The working class cannot simply lay hold of the ready-made state machinery, and wield it for its own purposes."[17]

Marx was writing in the wake of the crushing of the Paris Commune, which the terrified elites drowned in blood. The Commune was the first ever rising of the modern working class, who seized power in Paris after the government sought to disarm the working-class National Guard. The broad democratic changes ushered in by the Commune represented a first attempt and core framework for a workers' republic, and revealed deeper truths about what it meant to embark on a revolutionary road.

It showed that the state itself was not neutral but an instrument constructed for the rule of one class over another. The "lower" class could not hope to meet its needs against those serving as its antagonist simply by replacing them via elections. The structures predesigned to favor property and privilege of the exploiting minority had to be uprooted.[18]

> *'The working class cannot simply lay hold of the ready-made state machinery, and wield it for its own purposes.'*

In modern times, as we trace various forms of oppression and exploitation to their capitalist roots and their relationship to the state, this bears remembering. Our struggle is not to change laws but to overturn an entrenched power structure, part of whose fortress is the law itself. The only way to remake society is to uproot the institutions of elite power and replace them with institutions of popular and working-class power.

That means a new Constitution and new laws; new forms of decision-making in all aspects of society; new forces of public safety and community security; a new approach to law and order; and new armed forces to interact with the world's people on a completely different basis. None of that is possible without a new power—a revolution. ☐

The Soviet Union: Why the workers' state could not wither away

BY RICHARD BECKER

LENIN wrote "The State and Revolution" principally to recover the revolutionary essence of Marxism from those who had distorted it, especially the influential German socialist leader Karl Kautsky. The core argument of the work is that the state based on the class of exploiters must be smashed and replaced with a new state based on the rule of the formerly exploited.

In the latter part of the book, Lenin explained how this workers' state (constructing socialism, the lower phase of communism) would exist as a transitional stage towards a stateless society (the higher phase of communism).

Lenin wrote this as a general theoretical presentation, premised on the revolution occurring in one or more advanced capitalist countries in which monopoly capitalism had become dominant, laying the material foundation for socialism. He did not write it as a prescription for the Russian Revolution, which broke out months after he had completed most of the book.

At the time of his writing, Lenin could make use of one available historical example of the dictatorship of the proletariat—the Paris Commune—to make his case. Little did he know that within one year, he would be the leader of a new workers' state, formed under very different historical and social conditions.

Lenin had envisioned a relatively short period in which a Commune-style workers' state would defend the revolution and reorganize the economy on a socialist basis. Then gradually, as the revolution spread, social relations transformed, and growth of the productive forces reduced and then eliminated material scarcity, the state would wither away into the higher phase of communism.

In practice, the historical experience of the Soviet workers' state, isolated as it was and erected on the basis of great material scarcity, showed that, for it, the initial stage of socialist construction could hardly be easy or short. It took on enormous challenges—to rebuild and reorganize the economy and to defend the revolution from overthrow in a world still dominated by imperialist monopoly capitalism. Rather than the new state apparatus withering, a principal task of Lenin and the Soviet leadership in the first years after the revolution was to build up the socialist state to meet these challenges, while promoting the extension of the revolution through the Third (Communist) International.

> *It took on enormous challenges—to rebuild and reorganize the economy and to defend the revolution from overthrow in a world still dominated by imperialist monopoly capitalism.*

THE THEORY OF THE WITHERING OF THE STATE

In the chapter "What is to Replace the Smashed State Machine," Lenin outlined his views on how the workers' state would be radically different from earlier forms of the state:

> Capitalist culture has created large-scale production, factories, railways, the postal service, telephones, etc., and on this basis the great majority of the functions of the old 'state power' have become so simplified and can be reduced to such exceedingly simple operations of registration, filing, and checking that they can be easily performed by every literate person, can quite easily be performed for ordinary "workmen's wages," and that these functions can (and must) be stripped of every shadow of privilege, of every semblance of 'official grandeur.'

> All officials, without exception, elected and subject to recall at any time, their salaries reduced to the level of ordinary "workmen's wages"—these simple and "self-evident"

democratic measures, while completely uniting the interests of the workers and the majority of the peasants, at the same time serve as a bridge leading from capitalism to socialism.

These measures concern the reorganization of the state, the purely political reorganization of society; but, of course, they acquire their full meaning and significance only in connection with the 'expropriation of the expro-priators' either being accomplished or in preparation, i.e., with the transformation of capitalist private ownership of the means of production into social ownership.

Lenin drew on the 72-day experience of the Paris Commune of 1871, which the French bourgeoisie drowned in blood. Marx described the Commune as the first "dictatorship of the proletariat," the working class in power. The Commune replaced the institutions of the old exploiters, including the army and old bureaucracy, with new bodies accountable to the people.

Lenin explained the significance of this change. The Commune:

appears to have replaced the smashed state machine "only" by fuller democracy: abolition of the standing army; all officials to be elected and subject to recall. But as a matter of fact this 'only' signifies a gigantic replacement of certain institutions by other institutions of a funda-mentally different type. This is exactly a case of "quantity being transformed into quality": democracy, introduced as fully and consistently as is at all conceivable, is trans-formed from bourgeois into proletarian democracy; from the state (a special force for the suppression of a particular class) into something which is no longer the state proper.

While previous state powers had been built up and organized to defend the interests and property of numerically small ruling classes, the workers' state would be different. Because the working class was the social class with no private property and privilege to defend, its interests could only be served by the elimination of class divisions altogether. The workers would need a state to prevent

Winston Churchill, whose anti-communist, pro-imperialist views were so strong he advocated 'strangling the Bolshevik baby' during the revolution's early stages.

counterrevolution, but as this danger receded, and a new socialist culture and economy was built, the day-to-day necessity of the state would become superfluous and wither away.

Lenin believed that this process of transition could potentially begin immediately after the seizure of power, but would take place gradually and spontaneously rather than by a single act or order. It would coincide principally with dramatic changes in the relations between people, along with growth of the productive forces. As people were freed from the "horrors, savagery, absurdities, and infamies of capitalist exploitation," as well as from the privations of scarcity, they would over time accept the rules, norms and laws of socialist society "without force, without coercion, without subordination, without the special apparatus for coercion called the state."

SOVIET WORKERS' STATE CONFRONTS WAR AND INVASION

The reactionary capitalist and landlord Russian state was smashed by the October Revolution and the Civil War that followed, and a new workers' state brought into being. It was, in the beginning, more democratic than any previous state in history, with the possible exception of the short-lived Commune, in that it truly represented the interests of the vast majority of the population.

The obvious question raised by all of this is why the first socialist state did not in fact wither away. Why did it build institutions as extensive as any other state? It was out of necessity, once the decision was made to forge ahead with socialist construction even after it became apparent that socialist revolution was not on the near-term agenda in the imperialist West.

The revolution inspired millions of workers and nationally oppressed people around the world while at the same time horrifying the imperialists and the overthrown capitalists and landlords of the Russian Empire. Together they set out to "strangle the Bolshevik baby in its cradle," in the words of the infamous British imperialist Winston Churchill.

Within a few months of the triumph of the October Revolution, the newly formed Russian Soviet Federated Socialist Republic was under attack from 14 imperialist armies, which armed, funded and provided rear bases for the "White Army" forces serving Russia's capitalists, landlords and other reactionaries. Faced with this unprecedented assault by the imperialist powers and counterrevolutionary armies, the new Soviet government had to build up, as a matter of sheer survival, its military and civilian state apparatus.

Otherwise, it would have met the same fate as the Paris Commune. As historian Isaac Deutscher noted: "The government was formed, but few believed it would last ... most of them expected bloody suppression."

The counterrevolutionaries advanced rapidly, because at the time of the revolution the Bolsheviks had workers' militias but no real army. The old tsarist army, which had suffered millions of casualties during WWI, had—except for the White forces—mostly disintegrated and split. The vast majority of the population, after years of war, simply wanted peace. In these conditions, it would have been suicidal for the revolution to rely simply on workers' militias and the armed populace, as Lenin had predicted in "The State and Revolution."

Creating the Red Army became one of the immediate and essential tasks for the Bolsheviks. That they were able to build such an army and eventually win back most of the lost territory was a remarkable feat of history. Such a victory would have been unthinkable without the leadership of a dedicated Marxist party and the revolution's unleashing of the enormous energy of the working class and revolutionary peasantry.

That achievement exacted enormous costs, however. The Red Army suffered between 1.2 and 1.5 million killed, with millions wounded. Among the casualties were tens of thousands of the most dedicated and courageous communists, those who would answer every call to battle. These terrible losses took a great toll.

Building a modern army requires specialists trained in military science, something only possessed by those who have had military training. The Red Army had to enlist former tsarist military officers. Some joined out of sympathy for the revolution, some out of Russian patriotism, and many for pay and opportunist reasons.

All the Bolshevik leaders—Lenin, Trotsky, Stalin and the rest— were convinced that the Russian Revolution was just the beginning, the first of many other revolutions to follow, including in much more technologically and economically developed states, particularly Germany. They did not believe that their revolution could stand alone and survive.

Soldiers from the American Expeditionary Force Siberia, one of the many western military attempts to destroy the Bolshevik Revolution during the Russian Civil War

PHOTO: UNDERWOOD & UNDERWOOD

This vision of international revolution was not far-fetched. WWI ended not with a classical military victory of one side over the other—the war had fallen into military stalemate—but due to the eruption of revolutionary uprisings in Germany. Soldiers and sailors mutinied against their officers, and in city after city workers' or soldiers' councils—taking their inspiration from Russia's soviets—seized power in October and November 1918. The kaiser abdicated and a new republican government was established. But in the absence of a unified Bolshevik-type party, the reformist Social Democratic Party joined with the capitalist military command to suppress the potential socialist revolution.

There were, as well, mutinies in the French army and fleet, and even inside the British and U.S. occupying armies. Bolshevik anti-war and anti-imperialist agitation played an important role, and the spreading opposition to war limited the degree of intervention by the imperialist powers.

But still, in no country was there a successful revolution that could provide aid to the Russian Revolution. Even after withstanding Civil War and imperialist intervention, the threat remained of future wars and invasions.

THE ECONOMIC BATTLEFIELD
AND THE ONGOING CLASS STRUGGLE

The Russian Revolution's challenges were not just of a military nature but also economic.

By 1921, total production had fallen by over 85 percent from 1913, the last pre-war year. This was an economic collapse of unprecedented proportions among capitalist countries. By comparison, in the first years of the Great Depression—the worst economic downturn in U.S. history, which left tens of millions jobless and homeless—the decline was 46 percent.

To make matters worse, much of the capitalist world was still blockading Soviet Russia from all trade.

Key sectors of industry had completely shut down, dispersing the surviving industrial proletariat, which was the main base of the Bolsheviks.

In the heat of Civil War, draconian measures, which came to be called "War Communism," had to be implemented to prevent a complete breakdown of the economy and society. The measures included confiscating grain from the more well-off peasants needed to stave off mass starvation in the cities.

The peasants, who constituted about 90 percent of the population, had greatly benefited from the breaking up of the landed estates and the radical land reform carried out by the new government. But the extreme lack of industrial and consumer products to buy led millions of them to hoard their grain and other produce.

In order to restart the dormant economy, the party had to carry out a series of economic measures known as the NEP—New Economic Policy—that encouraged within limits capitalist production and trade. A layer of "NEPmen"—bourgeois traders—quickly emerged exacerbating inequality and posing the threat of a revived capitalism. About the crisis in 1921, Lenin commented on the negative consequences of NEP, while asserting that it was necessary to revive an economy that was nearly dead:

> Our enemy at the present moment and in the present period is not the same one that faced us yesterday. ... He is everyday economics in a small-peasant country with a ruined large-scale industry. He is the petty-bourgeois element which surrounds us like the air, and penetrates deep into the ranks of the proletariat. And the proletariat is de-classed, i.e., dislodged from its class groove. The factories and mills are idle—the proletariat is weak, scattered, enfeebled. On the other hand, the petty-bourgeois element within the country is backed by the whole international bourgeoisie, which still retains its power throughout the world.

In other words, social classes had not vanished just because a numerically small working class, supported by the poor peasants, had seized power. And instead of class distinctions immediately beginning to wither—and with them the necessity for a state—the Soviet workers' state had to, on account of the economic devastation, temporarily revive capitalist relations of production and distribution. This in fact facilitated the growth and influence of private-property-owning classes.

PHOTO: BERLINER VERLAG/ARCHIV

*Soldiers on the barricades
during the 1918 German Revolutiion*

Although there had been a socialist revolution, the class struggle was far from over; the difference was that the working class now
could wield state power against its class enemies. But even this possession of state power was largely indirect. Neither the productive
forces nor the educational and technical level of the numerically small
working class had developed to the point that rank-and-file workers
themselves could, in their spare time, manage the day-to-day administration of enormous industrial enterprises and the state's complex
relationships with peasant production. (Lenin's evolving views on
these challenges are taken up in the Addendum to this article.)

As with the military experience, economic specialists and man-
agers, largely taken from the old ruling classes and the ranks of the
previous tsarist bureaucracy, were called upon out of necessity. The
Communist Party attempted to absorb and direct these alien class
elements in the interest of socialist planning while simultaneously
expanding its base in the working class and training new specialists
from its ranks. As the party strove to control the state and government
bureaucracy—the real heart of the country's political and economic

affairs—it essentially merged with it, becoming the instrument of the "associated producers" in the fields of management and planning.

ISOLATION AND SOCIALISM

Horrific casualties in WWI and then the Civil War, the blockade, the collapse of the economy, the loss of so many communist cadre and the failure of revolutions in more economically advanced countries—all these factors profoundly shaped the process of socialist construction in the Soviet Union.

The failure of revolutions in the advanced countries had powerful objective causes, which in retrospect are much more obvious today than in 1917. The leading parties of the Second International had adopted the perspective of achieving socialism through gradual reforms and the parliamentary road. Eduard Bernstein and other reformist leaders based this perspective on the development of monopoly capitalism in the last half of the 19th century, which Lenin himself recognized as a major step, objectively, toward socialism. The reformist leaders wrongly concluded that the greater "organization" of the monopolies would lead to fewer and less severe economic crises and even end the drive toward war.

World War I, followed a few years later by the Great Depression and then World War II, refuted in life these reformist dreams. But Social Democratic parties had by now based themselves on a privileged layer of the working class and section of the middle classes that indirectly benefited from monopoly capitalism and imperialism with its super-exploitation of the workers and peasants of oppressed nations. Because of these privileges, these layers tended to lend support to imperialist policies and collaborated with capitalist politicians in suppressing and marginalizing revolutionary movements in the advanced countries.

These were the dire circumstances and isolation out of which the Soviet workers sought to build socialism. They could not wave a magic wand and transform these far-from-ideal objective conditions, nor was there any textbook from which they could draw to solve their problems.

In the absence of material aid from the advanced countries, even in the form of foreign imperialist investment, the Soviet workers' state was forced to implement "primitive socialist accumulation." This required appropriating from the peasantry through taxes, pricing of industrial goods versus farm produce, outright expropriation and other means to accumulate the surpluses necessary to industrialize on a socialist basis.

In the absence of material aid from the advanced countries, even in the form of foreign imperialist investment, the Soviet workers' state was forced to implement "primitive socialist accumulation."

In 1927-1928, with the economy largely recovered from WWI and the Civil War, a major new war scare—emanating especially from British imperialism—and increased hoarding of grain by peasants caused the Communist Party leadership to implement a major turn in policy. This involved bringing an end to NEP and greatly accelerating industrialization on the basis of the first of the Five Year Plans, coupled with a massive effort to collectivize and mechanize Soviet agriculture.

In the first several years, this shift in policy produced significant gains. But then, starting in late 1929 and early 1930, the super crisis that marked the beginning of the Great Depression hit the capitalist world. Agricultural prices on the world market, which had already dropped considerably from the heights reached during WWI, plunged. Prices of industrial goods also fell but not as steeply.

The first Five Year Plan required the sale of massive amounts of grain on the world market in order to purchase industrial and agricultural machinery. The impact on the Soviet economy was catastrophic. Far less machinery could now be purchased for a given

Soviet commisars

amount of grain exported, putting the whole plan of industrialization and collectivization of agriculture in jeopardy.

The response of the party leadership was to appropriate even more grain from the peasants in order to keep the Five Year Plan on track and to step up collectivization as a means to do so. Substantial numbers of peasants, especially in the "black earth" parts of western Ukraine, along with former NEPmen and sections of the bourgeois and petty-bourgeois intelligentsia, resisted these and other measures taken against private property and commodity trading.

The end result was what amounted to another civil war. The dominant section of the party leadership moved to further strengthen the socialist state, and in particular its repressive organs, to ward off counterrevolution and continue what would now become a forced march to industrialize in the face of mounting threats from Western imperialism and fascism. Major purges of the party and Red Army were carried out in subsequent years, culminating in the Moscow Trials of 1936-1938.

Then came WWII and Hitler's invasion of the Soviet Union, causing huge material losses and the death of 25 million or more Soviet soldiers and citizens.

THE END OF THE SOVIET UNION

Against what seemed utterly impossible odds, the Soviet workers' state survived for 74 years. Beyond survival, it became the second most powerful country in the world, leaped forward in the fields of education and science, and provided crucial aid to revolutionary movements and states for decades. Its survival and persistence reshaped the entire world order and global politics, checking and limiting imperialist ambitions while also providing the "enemy" that united imperialist forces as never before under the leadership of the United States in the post-WWII years.

The need for the Soviet Union to constantly struggle for military parity and survival introduced considerable economic distortions as massive resources were by necessity devoted to defense. It likewise introduced military discipline into politics. It created a vast bureaucracy that was largely insulated from and not accountable to the masses of people. The fact of public ownership of the means of production and centralized planning allowed for great feats on the one hand, but these distortions in the development of socialism left the Soviet bloc vulnerable to later crises of legitimacy.

This is what happened with the counterrevolution of 1988-1991, which was led by a section of the Soviet bureaucracy and party, and supported by an anti-communist nascent bourgeois layer of the Soviet society that was nurtured by a vast informal economy (also known as the "Black Market") which had grown up in the crevices of the planned economy. Counterrevolutionary forces from within Soviet society took advantage of economic and political reforms initiated by the Soviet Communist Party leader Mikhail Gorbachev to gain control over the media and parts of the government apparatus. They declared the Communist Party to be illegal and, with the assistance of all the Western imperialist powers, dismantled the socialist system.

The socialist stage is a transitional stage, not a completed process.

The socialist stage is a transitional stage, not a completed process. As an unfinished process, especially in a world dominated by capitalism, it was always at risk of transitioning back to capitalism rather than forward to communism. A complete and detailed explanation of why and how the Soviet state was overthrown is beyond the scope of this article.

Nonetheless, the momentous impact of the Russian Revolution and the Soviet Union on the world cannot be overstated, and key democratic gains of the revolution remain intact.

The revolution inspired and gave hope to the oppressed everywhere. It touched off the first truly global revolt of the oppressed and exploited in the capitalist world. It led to the creation of a new Communist International, unified as a single global working-class revolutionary party with member organizations in nearly every country.

It proved, above all, that the working class could take and retain power and reorganize society on a new socialist basis.

The overthrow and collapse of the Soviet Union did not invalidate the general principles or achievements of socialism. That historical experience simply represented humanity's first attempt at overthrowing and moving beyond capitalism. For that reason alone, all who are fighting capitalism today must study and learn from its successes and setbacks. □

Addendum

Lenin, the early Soviet Union and the Commune-style state

BY E.H. CARR

*Having withstood the brutal Civil War and a combined impe-
rialist offensive, could the Soviet government merely turn inwards,
snap its fingers and build the Commune-style state that its leadership
envisioned? Hardly. Some mistake this as a betrayal or abandonment
on the part of the revolutionary leadership of the "direct democracy"
spelled out in "State and Revolution."*

*E.H. Carr, a bourgeois but generally objective historian, addressed
this question in detail in his thoroughly researched three-volume
history of the first decade of the Soviet Union.*

*Rather than reinventing the wheel, we have reproduced an
extended excerpt from Carr's note "Lenin's Theory of the State."
Although not a Marxist, Carr's scholarship and findings are worthy
of close study.*

*Some paragraphs and block quotes have been broken up for
reading ease; the original footnotes have been compressed and the
sources updated with English titles, as Carr was working in the
Russian archives.*   —The Editors

IN *State and Revolution* [Lenin] invoked the example of ancient
democracy, where the citizens themselves were administrators.

> Under socialism, much of 'primitive' democracy will
> inevitably revive, since for the first time in the history
> of civilized societies the mass of the population will be
> raised to *independent* participation not only in voting and
> elections, *but in day-to-day administration*. Under social-
> ism all will administer in turn and will quickly become
> accustomed to nobody administering.[1]

It was in this spirit that Lenin praised the Soviets in September 1917 as the embodiment of a new state form in which a 'direct democracy' of the workers could be realized: 'Power to the Soviets'— this means a radical re-fashioning of the whole old state apparatus, of that apparatus of officialdom which puts the brake on everything democratic, the destruction of that apparatus and its replacement by the new, popular, i.e., truly democratic apparatus of the Soviets, i.e., of the organized and armed majority of the people, of workers, soldiers and peasants, the reserving to the majority of the people of initiative and independence not only in the election of deputies, but in the administration of the state, in the realization of reforms and transformations.[2]

It was in this spirit that he drafted his appeal 'To the Population' a few days after the October revolution:

Comrade Workers! Remember that you yourselves now administer the state. Nobody will help you if *you yourselves* do not unite and take *all the affairs* of the state into *your own* hands. *Your* Soviets are henceforth the organs of state power, organs with full powers, organs of decision.[3]

If bureaucracy was a specific product of bourgeois society, then there was nothing extravagant in the supposition that it would disappear when that society was overthrown.

The same principles applied to the management of economic affairs, of production and distribution. Lenin first expounded his views on this point in the pamphlet *Will the Bolsheviks Retain State Power?* written in September 1917. Apart from the repressive apparatus of the state 'there was also in the modern state an apparatus closely bound up with the banks and syndicates, an apparatus which performs a mass of accounting and registration'. This belonged to the category of the 'administration of things', and could and must not be destroyed; for this was a large part of the vital apparatus of the socialist order. '*Without the big banks socialism would be unrealizable.*' No difficulty need arise either in taking over the employees now engaged in this work or in recruiting the far larger numbers which would be necessary under the proletarian state, 'since capitalism has simplified the functions of accounting and control, reduced them to comparatively straightforward entries comprehensible to every literate person'.[4]

In *State and Revolution* he emphatically repeated this belief, and linked it with an eloquent vision of the process by which the state apparatus might be expected to die away:

> Thus, when *all* learn to administer and in fact independently administer socialized production, and independently carry out the checking and control of the boneheads, lordlings, sharpers and such like 'defenders of the capitalist tradition', then evasion of this checking and control by the whole people will inevitably become so immeasurably difficult, so rare an exception, and will in all probability be visited by such swift and condign punishment (since the armed workers are practical people and not sentimental intellectuals, and will not allow themselves to be trifled with), that the *necessity* of observing the uncomplicated fundamental rules of every human society will soon become a *habit*.[5]

How far were Lenin's views expressed on the eve of the revolution modified by the experience of the revolution itself? Its immediate effect was to quicken the belief in the possibility of an immediate transition to socialism. Looking back from the vantage point of 1921, Lenin confessed that in the winter of 1917-1918 the Bolshevik leaders were, without exception, swayed by 'presuppositions, not always perhaps openly expressed, but always silently taken for granted, about an immediate transition to the building of socialism'.[6] But before long the picture radically changed. During the winter the administrative and economic machine was running down at an alarming rate.

The danger to the revolution came not from organized resistance, but from a breakdown of all authority. The appeal in *State and Revolution* to 'smash the bourgeois state machine' now seemed singularly out of date; that part of the revolutionary programme had succeeded beyond all expectation. The question was what to put in the place of the machine that had been destroyed. 'The need to destroy the old state', Lenin told Bukharin in April 1918, was 'a matter of yesterday': what was now required was 'to create the state of the commune'.[7] Lenin had long ago laid down two conditions for the transition to socialism—the support of the peasantry and the support of a European revolution. The hope of realizing these conditions had been the ground of his optimism. The hope had not been fulfilled.

At home, the peasantry had supported the revolution as the power which had given them the land. But, once this was achieved, and now that the main demand of the revolutionary regime on the peasant was for the delivery of food to the towns with no visible prospect of an adequate return, the peasantry relapsed into sullen obstruction and even carried a part of the urban workers with them into an attitude of passive opposition. Abroad, the European proletariat still allowed itself to be led by its imperialist governments to internecine slaughter, and the first faint symptoms of revolution failed altogether to mature.

The new regime thus found itself isolated at home amid a predominantly indifferent and sometimes unfriendly rural population—the dictatorship not of the 'vast majority', but of a determined minority—and surrounded by a capitalist world united in its hostility to Bolshevism, though temporarily divided against itself. Lenin never openly admitted these disappointments, or perhaps even admitted them to himself.

But they were responsible for the apparent contradictions between the theory of *State and Revolution* and the practice of the first year of the regime. Lenin was faced with a situation in which the old state machine had been destroyed and the conditions for the building of the socialist order had failed to mature.

It was in these circumstances that Lenin sounded a first note of warning at the seventh party congress in March 1918. He resisted as premature Bukharin's proposal that the revised party programme should contain some description of 'the developed socialist order in which there is no state':

> For the present we stand unconditionally for the state; and as for giving a description of socialism in its developed form, where there will be no state—nothing

can be imagined about it except that then will be realized the principle 'from each according to his capacities,
to each according to his needs'. But we are a long way
from that. ... We shall come to it in the end if we come
to socialism.

And again:

When will the state begin to die away? We shall
have time to hold more than two congresses before we
can say, See how our state is dying away. Till then it is too
soon. To proclaim in advance the dying away of the state
will be a violation of historical perspective.[8]

A little later Lenin emphasized once more that 'between capitalism and communism lies a certain period of transition', that 'it is
impossible to destroy classes all at once', and that 'classes remain
and will remain throughout the epoch of the dictatorship of the
proletariat'.[9]

The Lenin of *State and Revolution* had thrown into relief the
prospective dying away of the state; and in January 1919 he believed
that 'even now' the organization of Soviet power 'clearly shows the
transition towards the complete abolition of all power, of any state'.[10]
But the Lenin of the years from 1918 to 1922 was more concerned to
dwell on the need to strengthen the state in the transitional period of
the dictatorship of the proletariat.

The most striking illustration of the change of emphasis was
found in the evolution of his attitude towards bureaucracy. In one
passage of *State and Revolution* he had already shown himself
conscious of the charge to which his sanguine expectations might
expose him:

To abolish bureaucracy at once, everywhere and
finally, cannot be thought of. That is utopian. But to
destroy at once the old bureaucratic machine and to begin
immediately to build up a new machine which will permit
of the gradual extinction of every kind of bureaucracy,
that is *not* utopian, that is the experience of the commune,

that is the direct matter-of-fact task of the revolutionary proletariat.[11]

Even before the October revolution he had written that it would be necessary to take the 'capitalists' and *compel them to work* in the new framework of state organization ... to put them to the new state service'.[12] During the next three years the period of the Civil War—the struggle for efficiency in administration, the fiasco of workers' control in industry and the discovery that in every field, from war to economic organization, the technical skills of the bourgeois specialist were indispensable to the working of the administrative machine caused him to beat a retreat from the conception of the management of public affairs by workers in their spare time. At the beginning of 1921, on the eve of the introduction of NEP, Lenin expressed himself in terms which read like an explicit repudiation of his own earlier position:

> Can every worker know how to administer the state? Practical people know that this is a fairy tale. ... The trade unions are a school of communism and administration. When they [i.e. the workers] have spent these years at school, they will learn, but it progresses slowly. ... How many workers have been engaged in administration? A few thousands all over Russia, and no more.[13]

It was this dilemma which, as Lenin confessed, had compelled the Bolsheviks, instead of destroying the old state machine root and branch, to take over 'hundreds of thousands of old officials, inherited from the Tsar and from bourgeois society, who work in part consciously, in part unconsciously, against us'.[14]

Faced with these difficulties Lenin returned the more persistently to his original antidote—the active participation of the rank and file in administration as the sole way of realizing democracy and countering bureaucracy. The process would be slower than he had hoped, but was all the more necessary:

> The further development of the Soviet state organization [he wrote in April 1918] must consist in every

member of the Soviet being obliged to undertake constant work in the administration of the state in addition to his participation in the meetings of the Soviet, and, consequently, in drawing the whole population individually and gradually both towards participation in the Soviet organization ... and towards taking a share in the service of state administration.[15]

In the last two or three years of Lenin's life the campaign against bureaucracy assumed immense importance, not only for Lenin the administrator, but for Lenin the political thinker. It was the practical expression of the campaign against state power of which *State and Revolution* had been the theoretical exposition. It provided the practical answer to the question how the state could in fact die away. This could happen only when every citizen was willing and able to shoulder his own share of the work of administration, simplified as that work would be when the 'government of men' had been transformed into an 'administration of things'. In the words of the party programme of 1919:

Conducting the most resolute struggle against bureaucratism, the Russian Communist Party advocates for the complete overcoming of this evil the following measures:

> (1) an obligatory call on every member of the Soviet for the fulfilment of a definite task in the administration of the state;
>
> (2) a systematic variation in these tasks in order that they may gradually cover all branches of the administration;
>
> (3) a gradual drawing of the whole working population individually into work in the administration of the state.
>
> The full and universal application of all these measures, which represents a further step on the road trodden by the Paris commune, and the simplification of the functions of administration accompanied by a rise in the cultural level of the workers will lead to the abolition of state power.[16]

It would, therefore, be a fundamental error to suppose that the experience of power brought any radical change in Lenin's philosophy of the state. The dying away of the state was in Marxist doctrine dependent on the elimination of classes and the establishment of a socialist order of economic planning and economic abundance; and this in turn was dependent on the fulfillment of conditions which had to be empirically determined at any given moment and in any given place. Theory could in itself give no ground for certainty about the right course of action or the prospect for the immediate future. Lenin could perfectly well admit, without stultifying himself or discrediting the theory, that he had miscalculated the rate of the process of transformation.

Nevertheless, it was also true that Lenin's theory of the state reflected the dichotomy in Marxist thought, which combined a highly realist and relativist analysis of the historical process with an uncompromisingly absolute vision of the ultimate goal, and strove to bridge the gap between them by a chain of causal development. This transformation of reality into utopia, of the relative into the absolute, of incessant class conflict into the classless society, and of the ruthless use of state power into the stateless society, was the essence of what Marx and Lenin believed. In so far as this was inconsistent, the inconsistency was fundamental; and there is no point in convicting Lenin, as is often done, of inconsistency of detail in his attitude to the state. ☐

Cuba's state in revolution

BY GLORIA LA RIVA

Nobody can deny that we made an army and that from the beginning we have inculcated gentlemanly and humane principles to that army. ... The armed institutions should offer services in peace, services to the people, services of a technical order. What we will not have is soldiers useless in barracks, nor with a "machete plan" and a weapon striking fear in everyone; what we must make is true soldiers who are an example, and who can offer all type of services to the country."

—Fidel Castro, Jan. 9, 1959,
TV program "Before the Press," Havana[1]

I WAS in Havana on a main street in 1993, during the depths of Cuba's Special Period. The country was undergoing enormous economic difficulties due to the collapse of the Soviet Union—Cuba's main trading partner—and the U.S. blockade.

I noticed a few police officers at the door of a bus that was stopped. There was loud conversation inside the bus among the passengers because the driver had refused to continue along his route.

The rule of no more than 45 passengers was breeched when too many people had boarded. The driver would not continue driving until some people got off the bus.

At that time, buses were extremely scarce due to lack of spare parts, tires and so on. Great care had to be taken of those buses that did function, including limiting the number of passengers on some buses.

The driver was trying to take care of the bus. And the passengers just wanted to get home after work. No one was about to sacrifice his or her ride home.

The police had come upon the situation and two of them were leaning into the doorway as they talked with the bus driver to resolve the standoff.

The most striking aspect of this incident was three young men, curious about the happenings, standing at the bus door, listening to the police and driver. They were right behind and next to the police, their hands on the police's shoulders as they leaned on them to get a better view of the incident. If the police had not been in uniform, you would have thought they were friends huddled together.

This small everyday encounter spoke to the relationship in socialist Cuba between the police and the people, of the mutual trust and respect and the lack of fear.

CAPITALIST VERSUS SOCIALIST STATE

Anybody in the United States knows that such an interaction would be impossible in our "democratic America."

In the United States, when police confront someone, especially Black or Latino youth, the cops warn bystanders and witnesses to stand far back or face arrest, brandishing their nightsticks or guns to make the point. Sometimes there is no warning.

Whether it is equipping police forces with combat gear to wage war on protesters, or gunning down youth with impunity, or financing town budgets through fines, filling the prisons to record levels, torturous punishment and isolation or the NSA's surveillance of every person's communications, the U.S. capitalist state has reached an unprecedented magnitude of repression.

The U.S. capitalist state apparatus protects a tiny minority of capitalists, bankers, landlords and the government in an inherently antagonistic relationship with the overwhelming majority, the working class and oppressed.

Socialism is the first system where the class that takes power is not a minority exploitative class, but instead represents the vast majority, the producers, the working class and peasantry.

And yet, class antagonisms do not simply end with the overturning of capitalism.

For Cuba—as in all previous and still-existing socialist countries—a state is essential to defend the people and the socialist gains. The armed forces, police, militias, courts and laws exist to protect the people against common crimes, to defend the Revolution against a return to capitalism and against U.S. imperialist aggression.

BATISTA'S RULE AND OVERTHROW

Fulgencio Batista was instrumental to U.S. domination in Cuba. He was Washington's man, first quelling the 1933 revolutionary struggle against dictator Gerardo Machado, then serving as president from 1940 to 1944 and ruling behind the scenes under other presidents.

Fulgencio Batista (left) and his wife at a meeting in Washington, D.C., 1938

On March 10, 1952, when it was clear his new presidential bid would be defeated, Batista launched a military coup, abolishing Congress and the Constitution and declaring martial law.

From then until Jan. 1, 1959, Batista's state machinery waged brutal attacks on the population through political persecution and massacres of students, workers and peasants opposed to his reign. More than 20,000 Cubans were killed at the hands of Batista's regime.

In the revolutionary war that began with the assault on the Moncada army barracks on July 26, 1953, the Rebel Army fighters were inculcated with a strict adherence of humane treatment toward enemy soldiers and the civilian population. When Batista's soldiers were captured, they were disarmed and released to return home.

With the revolutionary triumph on Jan. 1, 1959, the old army and police forces disappeared in the sweeping victory led by Fidel Castro.

The Rebel Army became the embryo of the new state and was instrumental in carrying out the early revolutionary measures of land reform and other economic decrees.

THE CHALLENGE OF UNDERDEVELOPMENT

What was the economic situation for Cuba's workers and peasants before the revolutionary triumph?

On Oct. 16, 1953, as Fidel Castro's trial concluded—for leading the heroic Moncada uprising—he gave a famous four-hour speech known as "History Will Absolve Me." He denounced the poverty and atrocious conditions that the people were forced to endure:

Eighty-five percent of the small farmers in Cuba pay rent and live under constant threat of being evicted from the land they till. More than half of our most productive land is in the hands of foreigners. In Oriente, the largest province, the lands of the United Fruit Company and the West Indian Company link the northern and southern coasts. There are 200,000 peasant families who do not have a single acre of land to till to provide food for their starving children. ...

Just as serious or even worse is the housing problem. There are 200,000 huts and hovels in Cuba; 400,000 families in the countryside and in the cities live cramped in huts and tenements without even the minimum sanitary requirements; 2.2 million of our urban population pay rents which absorb between one-fifth and one-third of their incomes; and 2.8 million of our rural and suburban population lack electricity. We have the same situation here: if the State proposes the lowering of rents, landlords threaten to freeze all construction; if the

Fidel Castro (center) delivering a political speech

State does not interfere, construction goes on so long as landlords get high rents. ...

Only death can liberate one from so much misery. In this respect, however, the State is most helpful—in providing early death for the people. Ninety percent of the children in the countryside are consumed by parasites which filter through their bare feet from the ground they walk on. ... And when the head of a family works only four months a year, with what can he purchase clothing and medicine for his children? They will grow up with rickets, with not a single good tooth in their mouths by the time they reach thirty; they will have heard 10 million speeches and will finally die of misery and deception.

THE SOCIALIST STATE AND REVOLUTIONARY MEASURES

The seemingly intractable poverty and suffering of the Cuban masses—amidst a sea of obscene wealth and sumptuous lifestyle of the capitalist class—was swiftly and decisively tackled.

Unprecedented economic decrees were publicly issued. One could wonder, how could such profoundly radical measures be enforced?

Simple. A new, truly revolutionary leadership had taken state power and began enacting a series of radical measures to benefit the working class and poor peasants. The enforcement of these measures was by the mass mobilization of the people, backed by the Rebel Army, which soon transformed into new institutions, like the National Institute for Agrarian Reform (INRA) and the National Institute of Housing and Savings (INVA).

By March 1959, utilities and housing rents were reduced by half, and evictions banned. Under the Urban Reform Law of 1960, half of the tenants soon became homeowners, and landlordism was eliminated.[2] Those persons with minimal rental property for personal income were given a pension. No one could own more than one primary home and a vacation home.

The great Agrarian Reform Law was signed on May 17, 1959. With land holdings limited to 1,000 acres, U.S. multinational capital in Cuba was dealt a mortal blow, and massive U.S. and Cuban-owned sugar plantations and cattle ranches were confiscated. Before the law, 15 sugar companies alone owned over 4 million acres.

In Cuba, nearly everyone owns their home.

A second land reform, in October 1963, further limited private ownership to 165 acres. By 1963, roughly 15 million acres were expropriated, a sweeping change in the balance of class forces across the island.[3]

The masses were the critical force in backing every revolutionary advance, with rallies of 1 million people or more to support the expropriations, especially in the face of dramatic U.S. economic aggression. The population of Cuba at the time was about 5 million. In turn, each new counter-measure by the revolutionary leadership bolstered the people's defiance of U.S. imperialism.

Almost all of Cuba's sugar had traditionally been sold to the United States for decades. In August 1960, U.S. Congress canceled the yearly quota of sugar purchases from Cuba.

In response, on Aug. 6, 1960, all U.S. sugar mills, oil refineries, the telephone and electricity companies were nationalized. On Sept. 17, the U.S. banks were taken over. By Oct. 24, all U.S. property was confiscated.[4]

DEFEATING U.S. IMPERIALISM

Within weeks of the triumph, U.S. imperialism had already decided to use military means to destroy the Revolution. The 1961

CIA-organized Bay of Pigs invasion was premised on the myth that the Cuban people would welcome the invaders as liberators and rise up against the revolutionary government. Within 72 hours, the mercenaries were routed, making this a resounding defeat for U.S. imperialism, April 19, 1961.

Meanwhile, the social progress advanced in leaps and bounds. Cuba became a "territory free of illiteracy" thanks to a nationwide campaign involving more than 100,000 young volunteers.

In February 1962, a trade and travel ban was signed into law by President John Kennedy, one of many U.S. laws that make up the U.S. blockade.

The proxy war was followed by Operation Mongoose, a U.S. plan for sabotage, assassinations, terrorist attacks and other measures aimed at overthrowing the Revolution. It was to culminate in a direct U.S. military intervention. This was prevented by the Soviet Union's sending of medium-range ballistic missiles with nuclear warheads to help deter the U.S. aggression and counterbalance the Jupiter MRBMs the U.S. had previously placed in Turkey and Italy, targeting the Soviet Union. This led to what is known in the United States as the Cuban Missile Crisis in October 1962.

Miami became a base of operations for Batista's exiles and other opponents of Cuba's revolution. Some 4,000 of the most violent elements—many of them former police and military officers from the Batista era—who left the island in the early 1960s were recruited by the CIA as shock troops.

Armed assaults soon began against the Cuban people, bombs placed in public places, assassinations of young literacy teachers and peasants, economic sabotage and biological warfare. Cuba's casualties from U.S.-backed terrorism are considerable, with 3,478 people killed and 2,099 permanently wounded.

To further protect the people from counterrevolutionary violence, a people's organization was needed: the Committees in Defense of the Revolution.

The CDRs were launched on Sept. 28, 1960, and organized block-by-block, with the residents 14 years and older joining to protect the neighborhood from sabotage and crime. There are presently 8.5 million members out of Cuba's 11.2 million people. The CDRs also coordinate volunteer work and blood drives, helping the

Civil Defense in hurricane evacuation, and participating in national days of defense preparedness, among other areas of work.

CUBA: A WORKERS' DEMOCRACY

The economic measures gave immediate benefit to the vast majority of Cubans. This factor, along with the constant political engagement of the leaders with the masses, helped solidify the radical and then socialist character of the Revolution.

For the first time in Cuba's history, democracy was truly exercised, even before a formal government and electoral process had been realized.

With Fidel Castro's declaration of the Revolution's socialist character on April 16, 1961—just hours before the Bay of Pigs invasion—the process of developing a formal government structure, elections and the Communist Party of Cuba (PCC), would soon begin and reach completion in 1965.

Cuba's ongoing revolutionary process and government are underpinned by a set of institutions that clearly provide participatory mechanisms and a level of engagement that continuously legitimizes the broad socialist path of the country.

First, there is the formal process of elections. Every two and a half years, elections are held for the country's 168 municipal assemblies and every five years for the National Assembly of People's Power and assemblies for the 15 provinces and special municipality of the Isle of Youth. All elected officials are subject to recall.

The National Assembly delegates elect the assembly president and vice-president as well as the 31 members of the Council of State. In between the National Assembly sessions, the Council of State assumes day-to-day responsibility granted it by the Assembly. The Council's president is the head of state and government. [5]

Elections in Cuba are by secret ballot, and candidates are nominated in neighborhood meetings directly as individuals, not as members of a political party. Everyone over the age of 16 is eligible to vote. The votes are counted in public, and a winning candidate must receive 50 percent plus one vote in order to win. If that percentage is not achieved, there is a second round. Cuba enjoys a high rate of voter participation, reaching 88 percent in the 2015 municipal elections.

PHOTO: NRYKKO

In Cuba, elections are open, free and fair.

The elections are completely free of campaign spending; no money is spent by the candidate. Instead, a one-page biography of each nominee is posted publicly about their record of service to the community. Nor do the elected delegates receive pay for their positions: Being a delegate is a volunteer service to represent one's district.

Unlike capitalist countries, there are no lobbyists filling the halls of Cuba's parliament, bribing legislators or writing the laws themselves, limiting unions' right to organize workers, or giving special tax breaks to giant pharmaceutical corporations, military contractors and so on.

Cuba's superstructure—the state apparatus, government, education system, elections, mass organizations—is based on the social and economic system of socialism.

With free, quality health care guaranteed as a universal right, everything derived from it—the training of 75,000 medical doctors, the biotechnology and pharmaceutical industry, the remarkably low infant-mortality rate of 4.2 per 1,000, and more—is based on the socialist incentive of providing health care to the people, not profits for stock investors. This example alone proves the superiority of socialism, and is all the more laudable given the U.S. blockade that has caused so much damage to Cuba's economy.

In addition to the CDRs, there are mass organizations like the Workers Central Union (CTC), the Federation of Cuban Women (FMC), the Union of Communist Youth (UJC), the National Association of Small Farmers (ANAP), the José Martí Pioneers Organization (OPJM) and more.

The CTC labor federation is composed of 20 national unions, the newest one representing the new non-state workers. Although labor unions in capitalist countries seek obligatory membership of workers in a union-covered workplace due to the overwhelming corporate hostility to unions, in Cuba union membership is completely voluntary.

Union membership among the Cuban workforce is extremely high, more than 95 percent, although there is certainly change in the percentage, since more than 500,000 people are no longer state-employed and their incorporation into other unions is an ongoing process.

The CTC's primary role is to defend and represent the worker in the event of any injustice or arbitrariness. It also works with relevant institutions in the implementation of the nation's economic plans and facilitates input from the workers into the plans. The CTC has direct input into any legislation dealing with employment.

As representative of the workers in a society where the government is not antagonistic toward the workers, but rather, is a gov-

Free, quality healthcare is a universal right in Cuba.

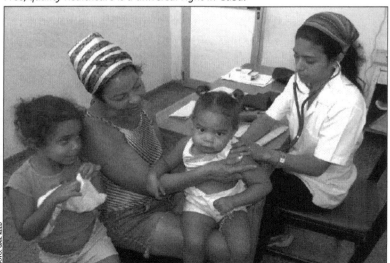

PHOTO: GAIL REED

ernment of workers' power, the National Assembly, the Council of Ministers and the CTC consult collaboratively to resolve problems for the betterment of the population.

POPULAR CONSULTATIONS

In critical moments of the last 25 years, major economic changes have been proposed that included a strategic shift toward foreign investment, tourism development and work reorganization. To explain the processes, receive input, make adjustments and seek consensus, all of Cuban society is brought into direct debate and discussion in the workplace and throughout broader society.

In 1993, the National Assembly deliberations were suspended and "Workers' Parliaments" were convened among the 3 million-strong workforce. Out of the 80,000 meetings, the workers formed the principal source of the debate on what would become the strategy to carry the whole people through the most difficult economic time in the Revolution's history: The Special Period in Time of Peace.

From 1989 to 1993, due to the collapse of the socialist bloc, the country's production dropped 34.5 percent and imports fell by more than 75 percent.[6] The national consensus and united resistance of the Cuban people through the extremely difficult years of the 1990s finally led to a recovery beginning in 1996.

Despite nearly unanimous predictions that Cuba could not survive the disappearance of the Soviet Union, it held on and has become an instrumental partner in the growing alliances among Latin American and Caribbean countries, an inspiration to millions worldwide.

The years 2008 and 2009 brought worldwide economic crises that have also deeply affected Cuba. The rise in the cost of food imports, along with a fall in revenue from exports such as nickel and sugar, and the need to grow Cuba's internal economy with more efficiency, productivity and self-sufficiency, required a deepening of the economic strategy that the government first embarked on in 1993.

The crisis was exacerbated by a series of highly destructive hurricanes that hit the island in 2008.

Once again, the people were fully involved in discussions at the workplace level, in what became the "Guidelines for the Economic and Social Policy of the Party and the Revolution," after tens of thousands of interventions. Much of the document—68 percent—was revised through popular consultation before its approval.[7]

Afterwards, an updated Labor Code, outlining the rights and responsibilities of workers and administrators, was proposed, debated and modified between July and October 2013, in 69,056 popular assemblies involving 2.8 million workers.[8] The code was approved by the National Assembly on Dec. 20, 2013.

The Cuban state operates in a way that seeks to build broad consensus under the leadership of the Communist Party. Hence the revolutionary government has been able to maintain, through constant communication and input, both direct and indirect, a close relationship with the broad masses of people, who clearly back the socialist direction of the country.

In spite of the many challenges and difficulties that Cuba and its people have faced over the years, Cuba's socialist revolution has enabled the Cuban people to create a remarkable society where health care, housing, employment, education, culture and social peace are rights enjoyed by all. □

Endnotes

Chapter Two: How the ideas of "The State and Revolution" changed history

1   Known as the Great October Socialist Revolution, started with a two-day insurrection on 25 October 1917 (by the Julian or Old Style calendar, which corresponds to 7 November 1917 in the Gregorian or New Style calendar).

2   Lenin, "The State and Revolution," p. 6

3   Sawer, Marian, The Genesis of State and Revolution, p. 215, 216, The Socialist Register, 1977, ed. Ralph Millibrand and John Saville

4   Nickolai Bukharin, submitted an essay; *Towards a Theory of the Imperialist State* in July 1916 for a series edited by Lenin, who rejected it for publication on the basis that it was erroneous. Bukharin published another version of the article in December 1916 under the title *The Imperialist Pirate State.*

5   Sawer, "The Genesis of State and Revolution," p. 217

6   Lenin, "The State and Revolution," p. 5

7   Lenin, "The State and Revolution," p. 32, Marx, Karl, The Eighteenth Brumaire of Louis Bonaparte

8   Letter to Joseph Weydemeyer

9   Marx and Engels, 1872 Preface to the German Edition of "The Communist Manifesto," p. 2, Struik, Dirk "Birth of the Communist Manifesto," p. 130, New World Paperbacks

10 Riazanov, David, Karl Marx and Fredrich Engels, An Introduction to Their Lives and Work, p. 198, Monthly Review

11 Ibid, p. 218

12 Sawer, "The Genesis of State and Revolution," p. 211

13   Nettle, Peter, "The German Social Democratic Party 1890-1914 As a Political Model, p. 78 Past and Present, No. 30, April 1965

14   Ibid

15   Becker and Majidi, "Socialists and War," appendix p. 41, Manifesto of the International Socialist Congress

16   Ibid, p. 46

17   Lenin, What Has the Trial of the Russian Social-Democratic Faction Proved?

18   Sawer, "The Genesis of State and Revolution," p. 212

19   Ibid, p. 211

20   Ibid, p. 216

21   Ibid, p. 4

22   Lenin, The Russian Revolution and the Tasks of the Workers of All Countries, March 12/25, 1917

23   Lenin, The April Theses, April 4, 1917

24   Lenin, "Several Theses," *Sotsial-Demokrat* No. 47, October 13, 1915

25   Ibid, Point 2

26   Evans, Alfred B., "Rereading Lenin's State and Revolution," p. 4 Slavic Review, Spring 1987, Vol. 46, No. 1

27   Lenin, The April Theses

28   Lenin, Meeting Of The Petrograd Soviet Of Workers' And Soldiers' Deputies, October 25 (November 7), 1917

Chapter Three: Living and cooperating without a state: studying pre-class society

1   F. Engels, "Origin of the Family, Private Property and the State" (International Publishers, New York, 1972), p. 181.

2   Richard Lee, "The Primitive As Problematic" (Anthropology Today, December 1993)

3   Mary C. Stiner and Steven L. Kuhn, "Changes in the 'Connectedness' and Resilience of Paleolithic Societies in Mediterranean Ecosystems" Human Ecology (October 2006)

4   Eleanor Leacock, "Myths of Male Dominance" (New York, 1981), pp. 139-140 as quoted in Chris Harman, "Engels and the Origins of Human Society" (International Socialism Winter 1994)

5   Richard Lee, "The !Kung San" (Cambridge 1979), p. 244, as quoted in Harman op. cit.
6   Stiner and Kuhn, op. cit.
7   Ibid., p. 703
8   Nicholas J. Allen, Hillary Callen, Robin Dunbar, Wendy James. "Early Human Kinship: From Sex to Social Reproduction" (Wiley-Blackwell, 2011)
9   http://www.chrisknight.co.uk/wp-content/uploads/2007/09/Early-Human-Kinship-Was-Matrilineal1.pdf; http://weeklyworker.co.uk/worker/970/anthropology-and-women-genetic-evidence-is-richer-/#8
10   http://www.chrisknight.co.uk/wp-content/uploads/2007/09/Early-Human-Kinship-Was-Matrilineal1.pdf
11   http://weeklyworker.co.uk/worker/946/anthropology-reclaiming-the-dragon/
12   Stephen Beckerman and Paul Valentine, "Cultures of Multiple Fathers" (University of Florida, 2002)
13   http://www.chrisknight.co.uk/wp-content/uploads/2007/09/Early-Human-Kinship-Was-Matrilineal1.pdf
14   Lenin, "State and Revolution," p. 467

Chapter Four: The U.S. state and the U.S. revolution
1   First was the Dutch Republic, followed by England.
2   Joseph Inikori, Africans and the Industrial Revolution in England: A Study in International Trade and Economic Development (2002 Cambridge) pp. 192-193
3   William Edgar Burghardt Du Bois, The Suppression of the African Slave Trade To the United States of America 1638-1870 (Harvard Historical Studies 1896)
4   Hence the so-called "Intolerable Acts" being the impetus for the First Continental Congress
5   www.rethinkingschools.org/static/publication/roc2/sla2roc2.pdf
6   https://armyhistory.org/the-battle-of-the-wabash-the-forgotten-disaster-of-the-indian-wars/; https://armyhistory.org/the-battle-of-fallen-timbers-20-august-1794/
7   http://clogic.eserver.org/1-2/allen.html
8   Chancellor Williams, The Destruction of Black Civilization:

Great Issues of A Race From 4500 B.C. to 2000 A.D. (1987 Third World Press) p. 362

9   Theodore W. Allen, The Invention of the White Race Vol. I-II (Verso 1994-1997); Phillip Alexander Bruce, Social Life in Virginia in The Seventeenth Century. An Inquiry Into the Origin of the Higher Planter Class, Together with An Account of the Habits, Customs, and Diversions of the People (Richmond 1902); Howard Zinn, A Peoples History of the United States 1492-Present (HarperCollins 1999) Ch. 2

10 Lerone Bennet Jr., The Shaping of Black America (Penguin 1993)

11 Gary Nash, "Black People in a White People's Country" in Stephen B. Oates et al, Portrait of America, complete ed., 8th edition (Houghton Miffilin Co. 2003)

12 Gerald Horne, The Counter-Revolution of 1776 (NYU, 2014)

13 This same sentiment is reflected in Lerone Bennet's Shaping of Black America cited above in Ch. 3.

14 Eugene Puryear, Shackled and Chained: Mass Incarceration in Capitalist America (San Francisco: PSL Publications, 2013), 36.

15 https://www.marxists.org/archive/lenin/works/1917/staterev/ch01.htm

16 One excellent study that reflects this general view is Leo Panitch and Sam Gindin, The Making of Global Capitalism: The Political Economy of the American Empire (Verso 2013); Another interesting study in this regard is Robert Allen, Black Awakening in Capitalist America (Africa World Press 1990)

17 https://www.marxists.org/archive/marx/works/1871/civil-war-france/ch05.htm

18 http://marx.libcom.org/works/1881/letters/81_02_22.htm

Chapter Five Adendum: Lenin, the early Soviet Union and the Commune-style state

1   Lenin, State and Revolution, Chapter 6. In other versions the word "administer" is translated as "govern."

2   Lenin, "One of the Fundamental Questions of the Revolution," Collected Works, Vol. 25, 370-377.

3   Lenin, "To the Population," Collected Works, Vol. 26, pp. 297-299.

4   State and Revolution, Chapter 3

5   State and Revolution, Chapter 5

6   Lenin, "Seventh Moscow Gubernia Conference of the Russian Communist Party," Collected Works, 2nd English Edition, Progress Publishers, Moscow, 1965, Volume 33, pp. 81-108

7   Lenin, "Reply To The Debate On The Report On The Immediate Tasks" in Session of the All-Russia C.E.C., Collected Works, 4th English Edition, Progress Publishers, Moscow, 1972 Volume 27, pages 279-313.

8   Lenin, "Speech Against Bukharin's Amendment To The Resolution On The Party Programme," March 6-7, 1918

9   Lenin, "Economics And Politics In The Era Of The Dictatorship Of The Proletariat," Lenin's Collected Works, 4th English Edition, Progress Publishers, Moscow, 1965, Volume 30, pages 107-117

10   CANT FIND

11   State and Revolution, Chapter 3

12   CANT FIND

13   Lenin, "The Second All-Russia Congress of Miners," Collected Works, 1st English Edition, Progress Publishers, Moscow, 1965, Volume 32, pages 54-68

14   Lenin, "Five Years Of The Russian Revolution And The Prospects Of The World Revolution: Report To The Fourth Congress Of The Communist International, November 13, 1922," Collected Works, 2nd English Edition, Progress Publishers, Moscow, 1965, Volume 33, pages 415-432

15   Lenin, "Ten Theses On Soviet Power" from the Extraordinary Seventh Congress of the R.C.P.(B.), Section Eighteen, March 6-8, 1918.

16   CAN'T FIND

Chapter Six: Cuba's state in revolution

1   El Pensamiento de Fidel Castro, Tomo 1, Volumen 2, (1983), p. 385

2   José Cantón Navarro, "History of Cuba: The Challenge of the Yoke and the Star" (2001), p. 215

3   James O'Conner, "Agrarian Reforms in Cuba 1959-1963" Science and Society (Spring 1968) pp. 169-172

4   José Cantón Navarro, "History of Cuba" p. 221
5   Silvia Martínez Puentes, "Cuba: Más allá de los sueños" (2003), p. 259
6   Felipe de J. Pérez Cruz, Cuba: utopias, realidades y posibilidades.
7   http://www.trabajadores.cu/20130224/a-esta-legislatura-le-corresponde-una-fecunda-e-intensa-labor-legislativa-en-el-fortalecimiento-de-nuestra-institucionalidad/
8   Susana Lee, "Conociendo el nuevo Código de Trabajo (I)", Trabajadores newspaper, Aug. 9, 2014.

The State and
Revolution
by V.I. Lenin

Preface to the first and second editions

THE question of the state is now acquiring particular importance both in theory and in practical politics. The imperialist war has immensely accelerated and intensified the process of transformation of monopoly capitalism into state-monopoly capitalism. The monstrous oppression of the working people by the state, which is merging more and more with the all-powerful capitalist associations, is becoming increasingly monstrous. The advanced countries—we mean their hinterland—are becoming military convict prisons for the workers.

The unprecedented horrors and miseries of the protracted war are making the people's position unbearable and increasing their anger. The world proletarian revolution is clearly maturing. The question of its relation to the state is acquiring practical importance.

The elements of opportunism that accumulated over the decades of comparatively peaceful development have given rise to the trend of social-chauvinism which dominated the official socialist parties throughout the world. This trend—socialism in words and chauvinism in deeds (Plekhanov, Potresov, Breshkovskaya, Rubanovich, and, in a slightly veiled form, Tsereteli, Chernov and Co. in Russia; Scheidemann. Legien, David and others in Germany; Renaudel, Guesde and Vandervelde in France and Belgium; Hyndman and the Fabians[1] in England, etc., etc.)—is conspicuous for the base, servile adaptation of the "leaders of socialism" to the interests not only of "their" national bourgeoisie, but of "their" state, for the majority of the so-called Great Powers have long been exploiting and enslaving a whole number of small and weak nations. And the imperialist war is a war for the division and redivision of this kind of booty. The struggle to free the working people from the influence of the bourgeoisie in general, and of the imperialist bourgeoisie in particular, is impossible without a struggle against opportunist prejudices concerning the "state".

First of all we examine the theory of Marx and Engels of the state, and dwell in particular detail on those aspects of this theory which are ignored or have been distorted by the opportunists. Then we deal specially with the one who is chiefly responsible for these distortions, Karl Kautsky, the best-known leader of the Second International (1889-1914), which has met with such miserable bankruptcy in the present war. Lastly, we sum up the main results of the experience of the Russian revolutions of 1905 and particularly of 1917. Apparently, the latter is now (early August 1917) completing the first stage of its development; but this revolution as a whole can only be understood as a link in a chain of socialist proletarian revolutions being caused by the imperialist war. The question of the relation of the socialist proletarian revolution to the state, therefore, is acquiring not only practical political importance, but also the significance of a most urgent problem of the day, the problem of explaining to the masses what they will have to do before long to free themselves from capitalist tyranny.

The Author
August 1917

The present, second edition is published virtually unaltered, except that section 3 had been added to Chapter II.

The Author
Moscow
December 17, 1918

Chapter 1

Class society and the state

1. THE STATE: A PRODUCT OF THE IRRECONCILABILITY OF CLASS ANTAGONISMS

WHAT is now happening to Marx's theory has, in the course of history, happened repeatedly to the theories of revolutionary thinkers and leaders of oppressed classes fighting for emancipation. During the lifetime of great revolutionaries, the oppressing classes constantly hounded them, received their theories with the most savage malice, the most furious hatred and the most unscrupulous campaigns of lies and slander. After their death, attempts are made to convert them into harmless icons, to canonize them, so to say, and to hallow their *names* to a certain extent for the "consolation" of the oppressed classes and with the object of duping the latter, while at the same time robbing the revolutionary theory of its *substance*, blunting its revolutionary edge and vulgarizing it. Today, the bourgeoisie and the opportunists within the labor movement concur in this doctoring of Marxism. They omit, obscure, or distort the revolutionary side of this theory, its revolutionary soul. They push to the foreground and extol what is or seems acceptable to the bourgeoisie. All the social-chauvinists are now "Marxists" (don't laugh!). And more and more frequently German bourgeois scholars, only yesterday specialists in the annihilation of Marxism, are speaking of the "national-German" Marx, who, they claim, educated the labor unions which are so splendidly organized for the purpose of waging a predatory war!

In these circumstances, in view of the unprecedently widespread distortion of Marxism, our prime task is to re-establish what Marx really taught on the subject of the state. This will necessitate a number of long quotations from the works of Marx and Engels themselves. Of course, long quotations will render the text cumbersome and not help at all to make it popular reading, but we cannot possibly dispense with them. All, or at any rate all the most essential passages in the works of Marx and Engels on the subject of the state must by all means be quoted as fully as possible so that the reader may form an independent opinion of the totality of the views of the founders of scientific socialism, and of the evolution of those views, and so that their distortion by the "Kautskyism" now prevailing may be documentarily proved and clearly demonstrated.

Let us being with the most popular of Engels' works, *The Origin of the Family, Private Property and the State*, the sixth edition of which was published in Stuttgart as far back as 1894. We have to translate the quotations from the German originals, as the Russian translations, while very numerous, are for the most part either incomplete or very unsatisfactory.

Summing up his historical analysis, Engels says:

> "The state is, therefore, by no means a power forced on society from without; just as little is it 'the reality of the ethical idea', 'the image and reality of reason', as Hegel maintains. Rather, it is a product of society at a certain stage of development; it is the admission that this society has become entangled in an insoluble contradiction with itself, that it has split into irreconcilable antagonisms which it is powerless to dispel. But in order that these antagonisms, these classes with conflicting economic interests, might not consume themselves and society in fruitless struggle, it became necessary to have a power, seemingly standing above society, that would alleviate the conflict and keep it within the bounds of 'order'; and this power, arisen out of society but placing itself above it, and alienating itself more and more from it, is the state." (Pp.177-78, sixth edition)[1]

This expresses with perfect clarity the basic idea of Marxism with regard to the historical role and the meaning of the state. The state is a product and a manifestation of the irreconcilability of class antagonisms. The state arises where, when and insofar as class antagonism objectively cannot be reconciled. And, conversely, the existence of the state proves that the class antagonisms are irreconcilable.

It is on this most important and fundamental point that the distortion of Marxism, proceeding along two main lines, begins.

On the one hand, the bourgeois, and particularly the petty-bourgeois, ideologists, compelled under the weight of indisputable historical facts to admit that the state only exists where there are class antagonisms and a class struggle, "correct" Marx in such a way as to make it appear that the state is an organ for the reconciliation of classes. According to Marx, the state could neither have arisen nor maintained itself had it been possible to reconcile classes. From what the petty-bourgeois and philistine professors and publicists say, with quite frequent and benevolent references to Marx, it appears that the state does reconcile classes. According to Marx, the state is an organ of class rule, an organ for the oppression of one class by another; it is the creation of "order", which legalizes and perpetuates this oppression by moderating the conflict between classes. In the opinion of the petty-bourgeois politicians, however, order means the reconciliation of classes, and not the oppression of one class by another; to alleviate the conflict means reconciling classes and not depriving the oppressed classes of definite means and methods of struggle to overthrow the oppressors.

For instance, when, in the revolution of 1917, the question of the significance and role of the state arose in all its magnitude as a practical question demanding immediate action, and, moreover, action on a mass scale, all the Social-Revolutionaries and Mensheviks descended at once to the petty-bourgeois theory that the "state" "reconciles" classes. Innumerable resolutions and articles by politicians of both these parties are thoroughly saturated with this petty-bourgeois and philistine "reconciliation" theory. That the state is an organ of the rule of a definite class which cannot be reconciled with its antipode (the class opposite to it) is something the petty-bourgeois democrats will never be able to understand. Their attitude to the state is one of the most striking manifestations of the fact that our Socialist-Revolutionaries and Mensheviks are not socialists at all (a point that we Bolsheviks have always maintained), but petty-bourgeois democrats using near-socialist phraseology.

On the other hand, the "Kautskyite" distortion of Marxism is far more subtle. "Theoretically", it is not denied that the state is an organ of class rule, or that class antagonisms are irreconcilable. But what is overlooked or glossed over is this: if the state is the product of the irreconcilability of class antagonisms, if it is a power standing above society and "alienating itself more and more from it", it is clear that the liberation of the oppressed class is impossible not only without a violent revolution, but also without the destruction of the apparatus of state power which was created by the ruling class and which is the embodiment of this "alienation". As we shall see later, Marx very explicitly drew this theoretically self-evident conclusion on the strength of a concrete historical analysis of the tasks of the revolution. And—as we shall show in detail further on—it is this conclusion which Kautsky has "forgotten" and distorted.

2. SPECIAL BODIES OF ARMED MEN, PRISONS, ETC.

Engels continues:

> "As distinct from the old gentile [tribal or clan] order,[2] the state, first, divides its subjects according to territory...."

This division seems "natural" to us, but it costs a prolonged struggle against the old organization according to generations or tribes.

> "The second distinguishing feature is the establishment of a public power which no longer directly coincides with the population organizing itself as an armed force. This special, public power is necessary because a self-acting armed organization of the population has become impossible since the split into classes.... This public power exists in every state; it consists not merely of armed men but also of material adjuncts, prisons, and institutions of coercion of all kinds, of which gentile [clan] society knew nothing...."

Engels elucidates the concept of the "power" which is called the state, a power which arose from society but places itself above it and alienates itself more and more from it. What does this power mainly consist of? It consists of special bodies of armed men having prisons, etc., at their command.

We are justified in speaking of special bodies of armed men, because the public power which is an attribute of every state "does not directly coincide" with the armed population, with its "self-acting armed organization".

Like all great revolutionary thinkers, Engels tries to draw the attention of the class-conscious workers to what prevailing philistinism regards as least worthy of attention, as the most habitual thing, hallowed by prejudices that are not only deep-rooted but, one might say, petrified. A standing army and police are the chief instruments of state power. But how can it be otherwise?

From the viewpoint of the vast majority of Europeans of the end of the 19th century, whom Engels was addressing, and who had not gone through or closely observed a single great revolution, it could not have been otherwise. They could not understand at all what a "self-acting armed organization of the population" was. When asked why it became necessary to have special bodies of armed men placed above society and alienating themselves from it (police and a standing army), the West-European and Russian philistines are inclined to utter a few phrases borrowed from Spencer of Mikhailovsky, to refer to the growing complexity of social life, the differentiation of functions, and so on.

Such a reference seems "scientific", and effectively lulls the ordinary person to sleep by obscuring the important and basic fact, namely, the split of society into irreconcilable antagonistic classes.

Were it not for this split, the "self-acting armed organization of the population" would differ from the primitive organization of a stick-wielding herd of monkeys, or of primitive men, or of men united in clans, by its complexity, its high technical level, and so on. But such an organization would still be possible.

It is impossible because civilized society is split into antagonistic, and, moreover, irreconcilably antagonistic classes, whose "self-acting" arming would lead to an armed struggle between them. A state arises, a special power is created, special bodies of armed men, and every revolution, by destroying the state apparatus, shows us the naked class struggle, clearly shows us how the ruling class strives to restore the special bodies of armed men which serve it, and how the oppressed class strives to create a new organization of this kind, capable of serving the exploited instead of the exploiters.

In the above argument, Engels raises theoretically the very same question which every great revolution raises before us in practice, palpably and, what is more, on a scale of mass action, namely, the question of the relationship between "special" bodies of armed men and the "self-acting armed organization of the population". We shall see how this question is specifically illustrated by the experience of the European and Russian revolutions.

But to return to Engel's exposition.

He points out that sometimes—in certain parts of North America, for example—this public power is weak (he has in mind a rare exception in capitalist society, and those parts of North America in its pre-imperialist days where the free colonists predominated), but that, generally speaking, it grows stronger:

> "It [the public power] grows stronger, however, in proportion as class antagonisms within the state become more acute, and as adjacent states become larger and more populous. We have only to look at our present-day Europe, where class struggle and rivalry in conquest have tuned up the public power to such a pitch that it threatens to swallow the whole of society and even the state."

This was written not later than the early nineties of the last century, Engel's last preface being dated June 16, 1891. The turn towards imperialism—meaning the complete domination of the trusts, the omnipotence of the big banks, a grand-scale colonial policy, and so forth—was only just beginning in France, and was even weaker in North America and in Germany. Since then "rivalry in conquest" has taken a gigantic stride, all the more because by the beginning of the second decade of the 20th century the world had been completely divided up among these "rivals in conquest", i.e., among the predatory Great Powers. Since then, military and naval armaments have grown fantastically and the predatory war of 1914-17 for the domination of the world by Britain or Germany, for the division of the spoils, has brought the "swallowing" of all the forces of society by the rapacious state power close to complete catastrophe.

Engels' could, as early as 1891, point to "rivalry in conquest" as one of the most important distinguishing features of the foreign policy of the Great Powers, while the social-chauvinist scoundrels have ever since 1914, when this rivalry, many time intensified, gave rise to an imperialist war, been covering up the defence of the predatory interests of "their own" bourgeoisie with phrases about "defence of the fatherland", "defence of the republic and the revolution", etc.!

3. THE STATE: AN INSTRUMENT FOR THE EXPLOITATION OF THE OPPRESSED CLASS

The maintenance of the special public power standing above society requires taxes and state loans.

"Having pubic power and the right to levy taxes," Engels writes, "the officials now stand, as organs of society, above society. The free, voluntary respect that was accorded to the organs of the gentile [clan] constitution does not satisfy them, even if they could gain it...." Special laws are enacted proclaiming the sanctity and immunity of the officials. "The shabbiest police servant" has more "authority" than the representative of the clan, but even the head of the military power of a civilized state may well envy the elder of a clan the "unrestrained respect" of society.

The question of the privileged position of the officials as organs of state power is raised here. The main point indicated is: what is it that places them above society? We shall see how this theoretical question was answered in practice by the Paris Commune in 1871 and how it was obscured from a reactionary standpoint by Kautsky in 1912.

"Because the state arose from the need to hold class antagonisms in check, but because it arose, at the same time, in the midst of the conflict of these classes, it is, as a rule, the state of the most powerful, economically dominant class, which, through the medium of the state, becomes also the politically dominant class, and thus acquires new means of holding down and exploiting the oppressed class...." The ancient and feudal states were organs for the exploitation of the slaves and serfs; likewise, "the modern representative state is an instrument of exploitation of wage-labor by capital. By way of exception, however, periods occur in which the warring classes balance each other so nearly that the state power as ostensible mediator acquires, for the moment, a certain degree of independence of both...." Such were the absolute monarchies of the 17th and 18th centuries, the Bonapartism of the First and Second Empires in France, and the Bismarck regime in Germany.

Such, we may add, is the Kerensky government in republican Russia since it began to persecute the revolutionary proletariat, at a moment when, owing to the leadership of the petty-bourgeois democrats, the Soviets have already become impotent, while the bourgeoisie are not yet strong enough simply to disperse them.

In a democratic republic, Engels continues, "wealth exercises its power indirectly, but all the more surely", first, by means of the "direct corruption of officials" (America); secondly, by means of an "alliance of the government and the Stock Exchange" (France and America).

At present, imperialism and the domination of the banks have "developed" into an exceptional art both these methods of upholding and giving effect to the omnipotence of wealth in democratic republics of all descriptions. Since, for instance, in the very first months of the Russian democratic republic, one might say during the honeymoon of the "socialist" S.R.s and Mensheviks joined in wedlock to the bourgeoisie, in the coalition government. Mr. Palchinsky obstructed every measure intended for curbing the capitalists and their marauding practices, their plundering of the state by means of war contracts; and since later on Mr. Palchinsky, upon resigning from the Cabinet (and being, of course, replaced by another quite similar Palchinsky), was "rewarded" by the capitalists with a lucrative job with a salary of 120,000 rubles per annum—what would you call that? Direct or indirect bribery? An alliance of the government and the syndicates, or "merely" friendly relations? What role do the Chernovs, Tseretelis, Avksentyevs and Skobelevs play? Are they the "direct" or only the indirect allies of the millionaire treasury-looters?

Another reason why the omnipotence of "wealth" is more certain in a democratic republic is that it does not depend on defects in the political machinery or on the faulty political shell of capitalism. A democratic republic is the best possible political shell for capitalism, and, therefore, once capital has gained possession of this very best shell (through the Palchinskys, Chernovs, Tseretelis and Co.), it establishes its power so securely, so firmly, that no change of persons, institutions or parties in the bourgeois-democratic republic can shake it.

We must also note that Engels is most explicit in calling universal suffrage as well an instrument of bourgeois rule. Universal suffrage, he says, obviously taking account of the long experience of German Social-Democracy, is

> "the gauge of the maturity of the working class. It cannot and never will be anything more in the present-day state."

The petty-bourgeois democrats, such as our Socialist-Revolutionaries and Mensheviks, and also their twin brothers, all the social-chauvinists and opportunists of Western Europe, expect just this "more" from universal suffrage. They themselves share, and instil into the minds of the people, the false notion that universal suffrage "in the present-day state" is really capable of revealing the will of the majority of the working people and of securing its realization.

Here, we can only indicate this false notion, only point out that Engels' perfectly clear statement is distorted at every step in the propaganda and agitation of the "official" (i.e., opportunist) socialist parties. A detailed exposure of the utter falsity of this notion which Engels brushes aside here is given in our further account of the views of Marx and Engels on the "present-day" state.

Engels gives a general summary of his views in the most popular of his works in the following words:

> "The state, then, has not existed from all eternity. There have been societies that did without it, that had no idea of the state and state power. At a certain stage of economic development, which was necessarily bound up with the split of society into classes, the state became

a necessity owing to this split. We are now rapidly approaching a stage in the development of production at which the existence of these classes not only will have ceased to be a necessity, but will become a positive hindrance to production. They will fall as they arose at an earlier stage. Along with them the state will inevitably fall. Society, which will reorganize production on the basis of a free and equal association of the producers, will put the whole machinery of state where it will then belong: into a museum of antiquities, by the side of the spinning-wheel and the bronze axe."

We do not often come across this passage in the propaganda and agitation literature of the present-day Social-Democrats. Even when we do come across it, it is mostly quoted in the same manner as one bows before an icon, i.e., it is done to show official respect for Engels, and no attempt is made to gauge the breadth and depth of the revolution that this relegating of "the whole machinery of state to a museum of antiquities" implies. In most cases we do not even find an understanding of what Engels calls the state machine.

4. THE "WITHERING AWAY" OF THE STATE, AND VIOLENT REVOLUTION

Engel's words regarding the "withering away" of the state are so widely known, they are often quoted, and so clearly reveal the essence of the customary adaptation of Marxism to opportunism that we must deal with them in detail. We shall quote the whole argument from which they are taken.

"The proletariat seizes from state power and turns the means of production into state property to begin with. But thereby it abolishes itself as the proletariat, abolishes all class distinctions and class antagonisms, and abolishes also the state as state. Society thus far, operating amid class antagonisms, needed the state, that is, an organization of the particular exploiting class, for the maintenance of its external conditions of production, and, therefore, especially, for the purpose of forcibly keeping

the exploited class in the conditions of oppression determined by the given mode of production (slavery, serfdom
or bondage, wage-labor). The state was the official representative of society as a whole, its concentration in a
visible corporation. But it was this only insofar as it was
the state of that class which itself represented, for its own
time, society as a whole: in ancient times, the state of
slave-owning citizens; in the Middle Ages, of the feudal
nobility; in our own time, of the bourgeoisie. When at last
it becomes the real representative of the whole of society,
it renders itself unnecessary. As soon as there is no longer
any social class to be held in subjection, as soon as class
rule, and the individual struggle for existence based upon
the present anarchy in production, with the collisions and
excesses arising from this struggle, are removed, nothing
more remains to be held in subjection—nothing neces-
sitating a special coercive force, a state. The first act by
which the state really comes forward as the representative of the whole of society—the taking possession of the
means of production in the name of society—is also its
last independent act as a state. State interference in social
relations becomes, in one domain after another, superfluous, and then dies down of itself. The government of
persons is replaced by the administration of things, and
by the conduct of processes of production. The state is
not 'abolished'. It withers away. This gives the measure
of the value of the phrase 'a free people's state', both as
to its justifiable use for a long time from an agitational
point of view, and as to its ultimate scientific insuffi-
ciency; and also of the so-called anarchists' demand that
the state be abolished overnight." (Herr Eugen Duhring's
Revolution in Science [Anti-Duhring], pp.301-03, third
German edition.)[3]

It is safe to say that of this argument of Engels', which is so
remarkably rich in ideas, only one point has become an integral part
of socialist thought among modern socialist parties, namely, that
according to Marx that state "withers away"—as distinct from the

anarchist doctrine of the "abolition" of the state. To prune Marxism to such an extent means reducing it to opportunism, for this "interpretation" only leaves a vague notion of a slow, even, gradual change, of absence of leaps and storms, of absence of revolution. The current, widespread, popular, if one may say so, conception of the "withering away" of the state undoubtedly means obscuring, if not repudiating, revolution.

Such an "interpretation", however, is the crudest distortion of Marxism, advantageous only to the bourgeoisie. In point of theory, it is based on disregard for the most important circumstances and considerations indicated in, say, Engels' "summary" argument we have just quoted in full.

In the first place, at the very outset of his argument, Engels says that, in seizing state power, the proletariat thereby "abolishes the state as state". It is not done to ponder over over the meaning of this. Generally, it is either ignored altogether, or is considered to be something in the nature of "Hegelian weakness" on Engels' part. As a matter of fact, however, these words briefly express the experience of one of the greatest proletarian revolutions, the Paris Commune of 1871, of which we shall speak in greater detail in its proper place. As a matter of fact, Engels speaks here of the proletariat revolution "abolishing" the *bourgeois* state, while the words about the state withering away refer to the remnants of the *proletarian* state *after* the socialist revolution. According to Engels, the bourgeois state does not "wither away", but is "abolished" by the proletariat in the course of the revolution. What withers away after this revolution is the proletarian state or semi-state.

Secondly, the state is a "special coercive force". Engels gives this splendid and extremely profound definition here with the utmost lucidity. And from it follows that the "special coercive force" for the suppression of the proletariat by the bourgeoisie, of millions of working people by handfuls of the rich, must be replaced by a "special coercive force" for the suppression of the bourgeoisie by the proletariat (the dictatorship of the proletariat). This is precisely what is meant by "abolition of the state as state". This is precisely the "act" of taking possession of the means of production in the name of society. And it is self-evident that such a replacement of one (bourgeois) "special force" by another (proletarian) "special force" cannot possibly take place in the form of "withering away".

Thirdly, in speaking of the state "withering away", and the even more graphic and colorful "dying down of itself", Engels refers quite clearly and definitely to the period after "the state has taken posses-sion of the means of production in the name of the whole of society", that is, after the socialist revolution. We all know that the political form of the "state" at that time is the most complete democracy. But it never enters the head of any of the opportunists, who shame-lessly distort Marxism, that Engels is consequently speaking here of democracy "dying down of itself", or "withering away". This seems very strange at first sight. But is is "incomprehensible" only to those who have not thought about democracy also being a state and, con-sequently, also disappearing when the state disappears. Revolution alone can "abolish" the bourgeois state. The state in general, i.e., the most complete democracy, can only "wither away".

Fourthly, after formulating his famous proposition that "the state withers away", Engels at once explains specifically that this proposition is directed against both the opportunists and the anar-chists. In doing this, Engels puts in the forefront that conclusion, drawn from the proposition that "the state withers away", which is directed against the opportunists.

One can wager that out of every 10,000 persons who have read or heard about the "withering away" of the state, 9,990 are completely unaware, or do not remember, that Engels directed his conclusions from that proposition not against anarchists alone. And of the remaining 10, probably nine do not know the meaning of a "free people's state" or why an attack on this slogan means an attack on opportunists. This is how history is written! This is how a great revo-lutionary teaching is imperceptibly falsified and adapted to prevailing philistinism. The conclusion directed against the anarchists has been repeated thousands of times; it has been vulgarized, and rammed into people's heads in the shallowest form, and has acquired the strength of a prejudice, whereas the conclusion directed against the opportun-ists has been obscured and "forgotten"!

The "free people's state" was a programme demand and a catchword current among the German Social-Democrats in the sev-enties. this catchword is devoid of all political content except that it describes the concept of democracy in a pompous philistine fashion. Insofar as it hinted in a legally permissible manner at a democratic republic, Engels was prepared to "justify" its use "for a time" from an agitational point of view. But it was an opportunist catchword, for it amounted to something more than prettifying bourgeois democracy, and was also failure to understand the socialist criticism of the state in general. We are in favor of a democratic republic as the best form of state for the proletariat under capitalism. But we have no right to forget that wage slavery is the lot of the people even in the most democratic bourgeois republic. Furthermore, every state is a "special force" for the suppression of the oppressed class. Consequently, every state is not "free" and not a "people's state". Marx and Engels explained this repeatedly to their party comrades in the seventies.

Fifthly, the same work of Engels', whose arguments about the withering away of the state everyone remembers, also contains an argument of the significance of violent revolution. Engels' historical analysis of its role becomes a veritable panegyric on violent revolution. This, "no one remembers". It is not done in modern socialist parties to talk or even think about the significance of this idea, and it plays no part whatever in their daily propaganda and agitation among the people. And yet it is inseparably bound up with the 'withering away" of the state into one harmonious whole.

Here is Engels' argument:

"...That force, however, plays yet another role [other than that of a diabolical power] in history, a revolutionary role; that, in the words of Marx, it is the midwife of every old society which is pregnant with a new one, that it is the instrument with which social movement forces its way through and shatters the dead, fossilized political forms— of this there is not a word in Herr Duhring. It is only with sighs and groans that he admits the possibility that force will perhaps be necessary for the overthrow of an economy based on exploitation—unfortunately, because all use of force demoralizes, he says, the person who uses it. And this in Germany, where a violent collision—which may, after all, be forced on the people—would at least have the advantage of wiping out the servility which has penetrated the nation's mentality following the humiliation of the Thirty Years' War.[4] And this person's mode

of thought—dull, insipid, and impotent—presumes to
impose itself on the most revolutionary party that history
has ever known! (p.193, third German edition, Part II, end
of Chap.IV)

How can this panegyric on violent revolution, which Engels
insistently brought to the attention of the German Social-Democrats
between 1878 and 1894, i.e., right up to the time of his death, be
combined with the theory of the 'withering away" of the state to form
a single theory?

Usually the two are combined by means of eclecticism, by an
unprincipled or sophistic selection made arbitrarily (or to please the
powers that be) of first one, then another argument, and in 99 cases
out of 100, if not more, it is the idea of the "withering away" that is
placed in the forefront. Dialectics are replaced by eclecticism—this
is the most usual, the most wide-spread practice to be met with
in present-day official Social-Democratic literature in relation to
Marxism. This sort of substitution is, of course, nothing new; it was
observed even in the history of classical Greek philosophy. In falsi-
fying Marxism in opportunist fashion, the substitution of eclecticism
for dialectics is the easiest way of deceiving the people. It gives an
illusory satisfaction; it seems to take into account all sides of the
process, all trends of development, all the conflicting influences, and
so forth, whereas in reality it provides no integral and revolutionary
conception of the process of social development at all.

We have already said above, and shall show more fully later,
that the theory of Marx and Engels of the inevitability of a violent revolution refers to the bourgeois state. The latter cannot be superseded
by the proletarian state (the dictatorship of the proletariat) through
the process of 'withering away", but, as a general rule, only through a
violent revolution. The panegyric Engels sang in its honor, and which
fully corresponds to Marx's repeated statements (see the concluding
passages of *The Poverty of Philosophy*[5] and the *Communist Manifesto*,[6] with their proud and open proclamation of the inevitability
of a violent revolution; see what Marx wrote nearly 30 years later, in
criticizing the *Gotha Programme of 1875*,[7] when he mercilessly cas-
tigated the opportunist character of that programme)—this panegyric
is by no means a mere "impulse", a mere declamation or a polemical

sally. The necessity of systematically imbuing the masses with this and precisely this view of violent revolution lies at the root of the entire theory of Marx and Engels. The betrayal of their theory by the now prevailing social-chauvinist and Kautskyite trends expresses itself strikingly in both these trends ignoring such propaganda and agitation.

The supersession of the bourgeois state by the proletarian state is impossible without a violent revolution. The abolition of the proletarian state, i.e., of the state in general, is impossible except through the process of "withering away".

A detailed and concrete elaboration of these views was given by Marx and Engels when they studied each particular revolutionary situation, when they analyzed the lessons of the experience of each particular revolution. We shall now pass to this, undoubtedly the most important, part of their theory. □

Chapter 2

The experience of 1848-51

1. THE EVE OF REVOLUTION

THE first works of mature Marxism—*The Poverty of Philosophy* and the *Communist Manifesto*—appeared just on the eve of the revolution of 1848. For this reason, in addition to presenting the general principles of Marxism, they reflect to a certain degree the concrete revolutionary situation of the time. It will, therefore, be more expedient, perhaps, to examine what the authors of these works said about the state immediately before they drew conclusions from the experience of the years 1848-51.

In *The Poverty of Philosophy*, Marx wrote:

> "The working class, in the course of development, will substitute for the old bourgeois society an association which will preclude classes and their antagonism, and there will be no more political power groups, since the political power is precisely the official expression of class antagonism in bourgeois society." (p.182, German edition, 1885)[1]

It is instructive to compare this general exposition of the idea of the state disappearing after the abolition of classes with the exposition contained in the *Communist Manifesto*, written by Marx and Engels a few months later—in November 1847, to be exact:

> "... In depicting the most general phases of the development of the proletariat, we traced the more or less veiled civil war, raging within existing society up to the

point where that war breaks out into open revolution, and where the violent overthrow of the bourgeoisie lays the foundation for the sway of the proletariat....

"... We have seen above that the first step in the revolution by the working class is to raise the proletariat to the position of the ruling class to win the battle of democracy.

"The proletariat will use its political supremacy to wrest, by degree, all capital from the bourgeoisie, to centralize all instruments of production in the hands of the state, i.e., of the proletariat organized as the ruling class; and to increase the total productive forces as rapidly as possible." (pp.31 and 37, seventh German edition, 1906)[2]

Here we have a formulation of one of the most remarkable and most important ideas of Marxism on the subject of the state, namely, the idea of the "dictatorship of the proletariat" (as Marx and Engels began to call it after the Paris Commune); and, also, a highly interesting definition of the state, which is also one of the "forgotten words" of Marxism: "the state, i.e., the proletariat organized as the ruling class."

This definition of the state has never been explained in the prevailing propaganda and agitation literature of the official Social-Democratic parties. More than that, it has been deliberately ignored, for it is absolutely irreconcilable with reformism, and is a slap in the face for the common opportunist prejudices and philistine illusions about the "peaceful development of democracy".

The proletariat needs the state—this is repeated by all the opportunists, social-chauvinists and Kautskyites, who assure us that this is what Marx taught. But they "forget" to add that, in the first place, according to Marx, the proletariat needs only a state which is withering away, i.e., a state so constituted that it begins to wither away immediately, and cannot but wither away. And, secondly, the working people need a "state, i.e., the proletariat organized as the ruling class".

The state is a special organization of force: it is an organization of violence for the suppression of some class. What class must the proletariat suppress? Naturally, only the exploiting class, i.e., the bourgeoisie. The working people need the state only to suppress the resistance of the exploiters, and only the proletariat can direct this suppression, can carry it out. For the proletariat is the only class that is consistently revolutionary, the only class that can unite all the working and exploited people in the struggle against the bourgeoisie, in completely removing it.

The exploiting classes need political rule to maintain exploitation, i.e., in the selfish interests of an insignificant minority against the vast majority of all people. The exploited classes need political rule in order to completely abolish all exploitation, i.e., in the interests of the vast majority of the people, and against the insignificant minority consisting of the modern slave-owners—the landowners and capitalists.

The petty-bourgeois democrats, those sham socialists who replaced the class struggle by dreams of class harmony, even pictured the socialist transformation in a dreamy fashion—not as the overthrow of the rule of the exploiting class, but as the peaceful submission of the minority to the majority which has become aware of its aims. This petty-bourgeois utopia, which is inseparable from the idea of the state being above classes, led in practice to the betrayal of the interests of the working classes, as was shown, for example, by the history of the French revolutions of 1848 and 1871, and by the experience of "socialist" participation in bourgeois Cabinets in Britain, France, Italy and other countries at the turn of the century.

All his life Marx fought against this petty-bourgeois socialism, now revived in Russia by the Socialist-Revolutionary and Menshevik parties. He developed his theory of the class struggle consistently, down to the theory of political power, of the state.

The overthrow of bourgeois rule can be accomplished only by the proletariat, the particular class whose economic conditions of existence prepare it for this task and provide it with the possibility and the power to perform it. While the bourgeoisie break up and disintegrate the peasantry and all the petty-bourgeois groups, they weld together, unite and organize the proletariat. Only the proletariat—by virtue of the economic role it plays in large-scale production—is capable of being the leader of all the working and exploited people, whom the bourgeoisie exploit, oppress and crush, often not less but more than they do the proletarians, but who are incapable of waging an independent struggle for their emancipation.

The theory of class struggle, applied by Marx to the question of the state and the socialist revolution, leads as a matter of course to the recognition of the political rule of the proletariat, of its dictatorship, i.e., of undivided power directly backed by the armed force of the people. The overthrow of the bourgeoisie can be achieved only by the proletariat becoming the ruling class, capable of crushing the inevitable and desperate resistance of the bourgeoisie, and of organizing all the working and exploited people for the new economic system.

The proletariat needs state power, a centralized organization of force, an organization of violence, both to crush the resistance of the exploiters and to lead the enormous mass of the population—the peasants, the petty bourgeoisie, and semi-proletarians—in the work of organizing a socialist economy.

By educating the workers' party, Marxism educates the vanguard of the proletariat, capable of assuming power and leading the whole people to socialism, of directing and organizing the new system, of being the teacher, the guide, the leader of all the working and exploited people in organizing their social life without the bourgeoisie and against the bourgeoisie. By contrast, the opportunism now prevailing trains the members of the workers' party to be the representatives of the better-paid workers, who lose touch with the masses, "get along" fairly well under capitalism, and sell their birthright for a mass of pottage, i.e., renounce their role as revolutionary leaders of the people against the bourgeoisie.

Marx's theory of "the state, i.e., the proletariat organized as the ruling class", is inseparably bound up with the whole of his doctrine of the revolutionary role of the proletariat in history. The culmination of this rule is the proletarian dictatorship, the political rule of the proletariat.

But since the proletariat needs the state as a special form of organization of violence against the bourgeoisie, the following conclusion suggests itself: is it conceivable that such an organization can be created without first abolishing, destroying the state machine created by the bourgeoisie for themselves? The *Communist Manifesto* leads straight to this conclusion, and it is of this conclusion that Marx speaks when summing up the experience of the revolution of 1848-51.

2. THE REVOLUTION SUMMED UP

Marx sums up his conclusions from the revolution of 1848-51, on the subject of the state we are concerned with, in the following argument contained in *The Eighteenth Brumaire of Louis Bonaparte*:

"But the revolution is throughgoing. It is still journeying through purgatory. It does its work methodically. By December 2, 1851 [the day of Louis Bonaparte's coup d'etat], it had completed one half of its preparatory work. It is now completing the other half. First it perfected the parliamentary power, in order to be able to overthrow it. Now that it has attained this, it is perfecting the executive power, reducing it to its purest expression, isolating it, setting it up against itself as the sole object, in order to concentrate all its forces of destruction against it. And when it has done this second half of its preliminary work, Europe will leap from its seat and exultantly exclaim: well grubbed, old mole!

"This executive power with its enormous bureaucratic and military organization, with its vast and ingenious state machinery, with a host of officials numbering half a million, besides an army of another half million, this appalling parasitic body, which enmeshes the body of French society and chokes all its pores, sprang up in the days of the absolute monarchy, with the decay of the feudal system, which it helped to hasten." The first French Revolution developed centralization, "but at the same time" it increased "the extent, the attributes and the number of agents of governmental power. Napoleon completed this state machinery". The legitimate monarchy and the July monarchy "added nothing but a greater division of labor"....

"... Finally, in its struggle against the revolution, the parliamentary republic found itself compelled to strengthen, along with repressive measures, the resources and centralization of governmental power. All revolutions perfected this machine instead of smashing it. The parties that contended in turn for domination regarded the possession of this huge state edifice as the principal spoils of the victor." (*The Eighteenth Brumaire of Louis Bonaparte*, pp.98-99, fourth edition, Hamburg, 1907)[3]

In this remarkable argument, Marxism takes a tremendous step forward compared with the *Communist Manifesto*. In the latter, the question of the state is still treated in an extremely abstract manner, in the most general terms and expressions. In the above-quoted passage, the question is treated in a concrete manner, and the conclusion is extremely precise, definite, practical and palpable: all previous revolutions perfected the state machine, whereas it must be broken, smashed.

This conclusion is the chief and fundamental point in the Marxist theory of the state. And it is precisely this fundamental point which has been completely ignored by the dominant official Social-Democratic parties and, indeed, distorted (as we shall see later) by the foremost theoretician of the Second International, Karl Kautsky.

The *Communist Manifesto* gives a general summary of history, which compels us to regard the state as the organ of class rule and leads us to the inevitable conclusion that the proletariat cannot overthrow the bourgeoisie without first winning political power, without attaining political supremacy, without transforming the state into the "proletariat organized as the ruling class"; and that this proletarian state will begin to wither away immediately after its victory because the state is unnecessary and cannot exist in a society in which there are no class antagonisms. The question as to how, from the point of view of historical development, the replacement of the bourgeois by the proletarian state is to take place is not raised here.

This is the question Marx raises and answers in 1852. True to his philosophy of dialectical materialism, Marx takes as his basis the historical experience of the great years of revolution, 1848 to 1851. Here, as everywhere else, his theory is a summing up of experience, illuminated by a profound philosophical conception of the world and a rich knowledge of history.

The problem of the state is put specifically: How did the bourgeois state, the state machine necessary for the rule of the bourgeoisie, come into being historically? What changes did it undergo, what evolution did it perform in the course of bourgeois revolutions and in the face of the independent actions of the oppressed classes? What are the tasks of the proletariat in relation to this state machine?

The centralized state power that is peculiar to bourgeois society came into being in the period of the fall of absolutism. Two institutions most characteristic of this state machine are the bureaucracy and the standing army. In their works, Marx and Engels repeatedly show that the bourgeoisie are connected with these institutions by thousands of threads. Every worker's experience illustrates this connection in an extremely graphic and impressive manner. From its own bitter experience, the working class learns to recognize this connection. That is why it so easily grasps and so firmly learns the doctrine which shows the inevitability of this connection, a doctrine which the petty-bourgeois democrats either ignorantly and flippantly deny, or still more flippantly admit "in general", while forgetting to draw appropriate practical conclusions.

The bureaucracy and the standing army are a "parasite" on the body of bourgeois society—a parasite created by the internal antagonisms which rend that society, but a parasite which "chokes" all its vital pores. The Kautskyite opportunism now prevailing in official Social-Democracy considers the view that the state is a parasitic organism to be the peculiar and exclusive attribute of anarchism. It goes without saying that this distortion of Marxism is of vast advantage to those philistines who have reduced socialism to the unheard-of disgrace of justifying and prettifying the imperialist war by applying to it the concept of "defence of the fatherland"; but it is unquestionably a distortion, nevertheless.

The development, perfection, and strengthening of the bureaucratic and military apparatus proceeded during all the numerous bourgeois revolutions which Europe has witnessed since the fall of feudalism. In particular, it is the petty bourgeois who are attracted to the side of the big bourgeoisie and are largely subordinated to them through this apparatus, which provides the upper sections of the peasants, small artisans, tradesmen, and the like with comparatively comfortable, quiet, and respectable jobs raising the holders above the people. Consider what happened in Russia during the six months following February 27, 1917. The official posts which formerly were given by preference to the Black Hundreds have now become the spoils of the Cadets, Mensheviks, and Social-Revolutionaries. Nobody has really thought of introducing any serious reforms. Every effort has been made to put them off "until the Constituent Assembly meets", and to steadily put off its convocation until after the war! But there has been no delay, no waiting for the Constituent Assembly, in the matter of dividing the spoils of getting the lucrative jobs of ministers, deputy ministers, governors-general, etc., etc.! The game of combinations that has been played in forming the government has been, in essence, only an expression of this division and redivision of the "spoils", which has been going on above and below, throughout the country, in every department of central and local government. The six months between February 27 and August 27, 1917, can be summed up, objectively summed up beyond all dispute, as follows: reforms shelved, distribution of official jobs accomplished and "mistakes" in the distribution corrected by a few redistributions.

But the more the bureaucratic apparatus is "redistributed" among the various bourgeois and petty-bourgeois parties (among the Cadets, Socialist-Revolutionaries and Mensheviks in the case of Russia), the more keenly aware the oppressed classes, and the proletariat at their head, become of their irreconcilable hostility to the whole of bourgeois society. Hence the need for all bourgeois parties, even for the most democratic and "revolutionary-democratic" among them, to intensify repressive measures against the revolutionary proletariat, to strengthen the apparatus of coercion, i.e., the state machine. This course of events compels the revolution "to concentrate all its forces of destruction" against the state power, and to set itself the aim, not of improving the state machine, but of smashing and destroying it.

It was not logical reasoning, but actual developments, the actual experience of 1848-51, that led to the matter being presented in this way. The extent to which Marx held strictly to the solid ground of historical experience can be seen from the fact that, in 1852, he did not yet specifically raise the question of what was to take the place of the state machine to be destroyed. Experience had not yet provided material for dealing with this question, which history placed on the agenda later on, in 1871. In 1852, all that could be established with the accuracy of scientific observation was that the proletarian revolution had approached the task of "concentrating all its forces of destruction" against the state power, of "smashing" the state machine.

Here the question may arise: is it correct to generalize the experience, observations and conclusions of Marx, to apply them to a field that is wider than the history of France during the three years 1848-51? Before proceeding to deal with this question, let us recall a remark made by Engels and then examine the facts. In his introduction to the third edition of *The Eighteenth Brumaire*, Engels wrote:

> "France is the country where, more than anywhere else, the historical class struggles were each time fought out to a finish, and where, consequently, the changing political forms within which they move and in which their results are summarized have been stamped in the sharpest outlines. The centre of feudalism in the Middle Ages, the model country, since the Renaissance, of a unified monarchy based on social estates, France demolished feudalism in the Great Revolution and established the rule of the bourgeoisie in a classical purity unequalled by any other European land. And the struggle of the upward-striving proletariat against the ruling bourgeoisie appeared here in an acute form unknown elsewhere." (p.4, 1907 edition)

The last remark is out of date insomuch as since 1871 there has been a lull in the revolutionary struggle of the French proletariat, although, long as this lull may be, it does not at all preclude the possibility that in the coming proletarian revolution France may show herself to be the classic country of the class struggle to a finish.

Let us, however, cast a general glance over the history of the advanced countries at the turn of the century. We shall see that the same process went on more slowly, in more varied forms, in a much wider field: on the one hand, the development of "parliamentary power" both in the republican countries (France, America, Switzerland), and in the monarchies (Britain, Germany to a certain extent, Italy, the Scandinavia countries, etc.); on the other hand, a struggle for power among the various bourgeois and petty-bourgeois parties which distributed and redistributed the "spoils" of office, with the foundations of bourgeois society unchanged; and, lastly, the perfection and consolidation of the "executive power", of its bureaucratic and military apparatus.

There is not the slightest doubt that these features are common to the whole of the modern evolution of all capitalist states in general. In the last three years 1848-51 France displayed, in a swift, sharp, concentrated form, the very same processes of development which are peculiar to the whole capitalist world.

Imperialism—the era of bank capital, the era of gigantic capitalist monopolies, of the development of monopoly capitalism into state-monopoly capitalism—has clearly shown an unprecedented growth in its bureaucratic and military apparatus in connection with the intensification of repressive measures against the proletariat both in the monarchical and in the freest, republican countries.

World history is now undoubtedly leading, on an incomparably larger scale than in 1852, to the "concentration of all the forces" of the proletarian revolution on the "destruction" of the state machine.

What the proletariat will put in its place is suggested by the highly instructive material furnished by the Paris Commune.

3. THE PRESENTATION OF THE QUESTION BY MARX IN 1852

In 1907, Mehring, in the magazine *Neue Zeit*[4] (Vol.XXV, 2, p.164), published extracts from Marx's letter to Weydemeyer dated March 5, 1852. This letter, among other things, contains the following remarkable observation:

> "And now as to myself, no credit is due to me for discovering the existence of classes in modern society or the struggle between them. Long before me bourgeois historians had described the historical development of this class struggle and bourgeois economists, the economic anatomy of classes. What I did that was new was to prove: (1) that the existence of classes is only bound up with the particular, historical phases in the development of production (historische Entwicklungsphasen der Produktion), (2) that the class struggle necessarily leads to the dictatorship of the proletariat, (3) that this dictatorship itself only constitutes the transition to the abolition of all classes and to a classless society."[5]

In these words, Marx succeeded in expressing with striking clarity, first, the chief and radical difference between his theory and that of the foremost and most profound thinkers of the bourgeoisie; and, secondly, the essence of his theory of the state.

It is often said and written that the main point in Marx's theory is the class struggle. But this is wrong. And this wrong notion very often results in an opportunist distortion of Marxism and its falsification in a spirit acceptable to the bourgeoisie. For the theory of the class struggle was created not by Marx, but by the bourgeoisie before Marx, and, generally speaking, it is acceptable to the bourgeoisie. Those who recognize only the class struggle are not yet Marxists; they may be found to be still within the bounds of bourgeois thinking and bourgeois politics. To confine Marxism to the theory of the class struggle means curtailing Marxism, distorting it, reducing it to something acceptable to the bourgeoisie. Only he is a Marxist who extends the recognition of the class struggle to the recognition of the dictatorship of the proletariat. That is what constitutes the most profound distinction between the Marxist and the ordinary petty (as well as big) bourgeois. This is the touchstone on which the real understanding and recognition of Marxism should be tested. And it is not surprising that when the history of Europe brought the working class face to face with this question as a practical issue, not only all the opportunists and reformists, but all the Kautskyites (people who vacillate between reformism and Marxism) proved to be miserable philistines and petty-bourgeois democrats repudiating the dictatorship of the proletariat. Kautsky's pamphlet, *The Dictatorship of the Proletariat*, published in August 1918, i.e., long after the first edition of the present book, is a perfect example of petty-bourgeois distortion of Marxism and base renunciation of it in deeds, while hypocritically recognizing it in words (see my pamphlet, *The Proletarian Revolution and the Renegade Kautsky*, Petrograd and Moscow, 1918).

Opportunism today, as represented by its principal spokesman, the ex-Marxist Karl Kautsky, fits in completely with Marx's characterization of the bourgeois position quoted above, for this opportunism limits recognition of the class struggle to the sphere of bourgeois relations. (Within this sphere, within its framework, not a single educated liberal will refuse to recognize the class struggle "in principle"!) Opportunism does not extend recognition of the class struggle to the cardinal point, to the period of transition from capitalism to communism, of the overthrow and the complete abolition of the bourgeoisie. In reality, this period inevitably is a period of an unprecedently violent class struggle in unprecedentedly acute forms, and, consequently, during this period the state must inevitably be a state that is democratic in a new way (for the proletariat and the propertyless in general) and dictatorial in a new way (against the bourgeoisie).

Further. The essence of Marx's theory of the state has been mastered only by those who realize that the dictatorship of a single class is necessary not only for every class society in general, not only for the proletariat which has overthrown the bourgeoisie, but also for the entire historical period which separates capitalism from "classless society", from communism. Bourgeois states are most varied in form, but their essence is the same: all these states, whatever their form, in the final analysis are inevitably the dictatorship of the bourgeoisie. The transition from capitalism to communism is certainly bound to yield a tremendous abundance and variety of political forms, but the essence will inevitably be the same: the dictatorship of the proletariat. □

Chapter 3

Experience of the Paris Commune of 1871. Marx's analysis

1. WHAT MADE THE COMMUNARDS' ATTEMPT HEROIC?

IT is well known that in the autumn of 1870, a few months before the Commune, Marx warned the Paris workers that any attempt to overthrow the government would be the folly of despair. But when, in March 1871, a decisive battle was forced upon the workers and they accepted it, when the uprising had become a fact, Marx greeted the proletarian revolution with the greatest enthusiasm, in spite of unfavorable auguries. Marx did not persist in the pedantic attitude of condemning an "untimely" movement as did the ill-famed Russian renegade from marxism, Plekhanov, who in November 1905 wrote encouragingly about the workers' and peasants' struggle, but after December 1905 cried, liberal fashion: "They should not have taken up arms."

Marx, however, was not only enthusiastic about the heroism of the Communards, who, as he expressed it, "stormed heaven". Although the mass revolutionary movement did not achieve its aim, he regarded it as a historic experience of enormous importance, as a certain advance of the world proletarian revolution, as a practical step that was more important than hundreds of programmes and arguments. Marx endeavored to analyze this experiment, to draw tactical lessons from it and re-examine his theory in the light of it.

The only "correction" Marx thought it necessary to make to the *Communist Manifesto* he made on the basis of the revolutionary experience of the Paris Commune.

The last preface to the new German edition of the *Communist Manifesto*, signed by both its authors, is dated June 24, 1872. In this preface the authors, Karl Marx and Frederick Engels, say that the programme of the *Communist Manifesto* "has in some details become out-of-date", and the go on to say:

> "... One thing especially was proved by the Commune, viz., that 'the working class cannot simply lay hold of the ready-made state machinery and wield it for its own purposes'...."[1]

The authors took the words that are in single quotation marks in this passage from Marx's book, *The Civil War in France*.

Thus, Marx and Engels regarded one principal and fundamental lesson of the Paris Commune as being of such enormous importance that they introduced it as an important correction into the *Communist Manifesto*.

Most characteristically, it is this important correction that has been distorted by the opportunists, and its meaning probably is not known to nine-tenths, if not ninety-nine-hundredths, of the readers of the *Communist Manifesto*. We shall deal with this distortion more fully farther on, in a chapter devoted specially to distortions. Here it will be sufficient to note that the current, vulgar "interpretation" of Marx's famous statement just quoted is that Marx here allegedly emphasizes the idea of slow development in contradistinction to the seizure of power, and so on.

As a matter of fact, the exact opposite is the case. Marx's idea is that the working class must break up, smash the "ready-made state machinery", and not confine itself merely to laying hold of it.

On April 12, 1871, i.e., just at the time of the Commune, Marx wrote to Kugelmann:

> "If you look up the last chapter of my *Eighteenth Brumaire*, you will find that I declare that the next attempt of the French Revolution will be no longer, as before, to transfer the bureaucratic-military machine from one hand to another, but to *smash* it [Marx's italics—the original is *zerbrechen*], and this is the precondition for every real people's revolution on the Continent. And this is what our heroic Party comrades in Paris are attempting." (*Neue Zeit*, Vol.XX, 1, 1901-02, p. 709.)[2]

(The letters of Marx to Kugelmann have appeared in Russian in no less than two editions, one of which I edited and supplied with a preface.)

The words, "to smash the bureaucratic-military machine", briefly express the principal lesson of Marxism regarding the tasks of the proletariat during a revolution in relation to the state. And this is the lesson that has been not only completely ignored, but positively distorted by the prevailing, Kautskyite, "interpretation" of Marxism!

As for Marx's reference to *The Eighteenth Brumaire*, we have quoted the relevant passage in full above.

It is interesting to note, in particular, two points in the above-quoted argument of Marx. First, he restricts his conclusion to the Continent. This was understandable in 1871, when Britain was still the model of a purely capitalist country, but without a militarist clique and, to a considerable degree, without a bureaucracy. Marx therefore excluded Britain, where a revolution, even a people's revolution, then seemed possible, and indeed was possible, *without* the precondition of destroying "ready-made state machinery".

Today, in 1917, at the time of the first great imperialist war, this restriction made by Marx is no longer valid. Both Britain and America, the biggest and the last representatives—in the whole world—of Anglo-Saxon "liberty", in the sense that they had no militarist cliques and bureaucracy, have completely sunk into the all-European filthy, bloody morass of bureaucratic-military institutions which subordinate everything to themselves, and suppress everything. Today, in Britain and America, too, "the precondition for every real people's revolution" is the *smashing*, the *destruction* of the "ready-made state machinery" (made and brought up to the "European", general imperialist, perfection in those countries in the years 1914-17).

Secondly, particular attention should be paid to Marx's extremely profound remark that the destruction of the bureaucratic-military state machine is "the precondition for every real *people's* revolution". This idea of a "people's revolution seems strange coming from Marx, so that the Russian Plekhanovites and Mensheviks, those followers of Struve who wish to be regarded as Marxists, might possibly declare such an expression to be a "slip of the pen" on Marx's part. They have reduced Marxism to such a state of wretchedly liberal distortion that nothing exists for them beyond the antithesis between bourgeois revolution and proletarian revolution, and even this antithesis they interpret in an utterly lifeless way.

If we take the revolutions of the 20th century as examples we shall, of course, have to admit that the Portuguese and the Turkish revolutions are both bourgeois revolutions. Neither of them, however, is a "people's" revolution, since in neither does the mass of the people, their vast majority, come out actively, independently, with their own economic and political demands to any noticeable degree. By contrast, although the Russian bourgeois revolution of 1905-07 displayed no such "brilliant" successes as at time fell to the Portuguese and Turkish revolutions, it was undoubtedly a "real people's" revolution, since the mass of the people, their majority, the very lowest social groups, crushed by oppression and exploitation, rose independently and stamped on the entire course of the revolution the imprint of *their* own demands, *their* attempt to build in their own way a new society in place of the old society that was being destroyed.

In Europe, in 1871, the proletariat did not constitute the majority of the people in any country on the Continent. A "people's" revolution, one actually sweeping the majority into its stream, could be such only if it embraced both the proletariat and the peasants. These two classes then constituted the "people". These two classes are united by the fact that the "bureaucratic-military state machine" oppresses, crushes, exploits them. To *smash* this machine, *to break it up*, is truly in the interest of the "people", of their majority, of the workers and most of the peasants, is "the precondition" for a free alliance of the poor peasant and the proletarians, whereas without such an alliance democracy is unstable and socialist transformation is impossible.

As is well known, the Paris Commune was actually working its way toward such an alliance, although it did not reach its goal owing to a number of circumstances, internal and external.

Consequently, in speaking of a "real people's revolution", Marx, without in the least discounting the special features of the petty bourgeois (he spoke a great deal about them and often), took strict account of the actual balance of class forces in most of the continental countries of Europe in 1871. On the other hand, he stated that the "smashing" of the state machine was required by the interests of both the workers and the peasants, that it united them, that it placed before them the common task of removing the "parasite" and of replacing it by something new.

By what exactly?

2. WHAT IS TO REPLACE THE SMASHED STATE MACHINE?

In 1847, in the *Communist Manifesto*, Marx's answer to this question was as yet a purely abstract one; to be exact, it was an answer that indicated he tasks, but not the ways of accomplishing them. The answer given in the *Communist Manifesto* was that this machine was to be replaced by "the proletariat organized as the ruling class", by the "winning of the battle of democracy".

Marx did not indulge in utopias; he expected the experience of the mass movement to provide the reply to the question as to the specific forms this organisation of the proletariat as the ruling class would assume and as to the exact manner in which this organisation would be combined with the most complete, most consistent "winning of the battle of democracy."

Marx subjected the experience of the Commune, meagre as it was, to the most careful analysis in *The Civil War in France*. Let us quote the most important passages of this work. [All the following quotes in this Chapter, with one exception, are so cited–Ed.]

Originating from the Middle Ages, there developed in the 19th century "the centralized state power, with its ubiquitous organs of standing army, police, bureaucracy, clergy, and judicature." With the development of class antagonisms between capital and labor, "state power assumed more and more the character of a public force organized for the suppression of the working class, of a machine of class rule. After every revolution, which marks an advance in the class struggle, the purely coercive character of the state power stands out in bolder and bolder relief." After the revolution of 1848-49, state power became "the national war instruments of capital against labor". The Second Empire consolidated this.

"The direct antithesis to the empire was the Commune." It was the "specific form" of "a republic that was not only to remove the monarchical form of class rule, but class rule itself."

What was this "specific" form of the proletarian, socialist republic? What was the state it began to create?

"The first decree of the Commune, therefore, was the suppression of the standing army, and the substitution for it of the armed people."

This demand now figures in the programme of every party calling itself socialist. The real worth of their programme, however, is best shown by the behavior of our Social-Revolutionists and Mensheviks, who, right after the revolution of February 27, refused to carry out this demand!

"The Commune was formed of the municipal councillors, chosen by universal suffrage in the various wards of the town, responsible and revocable at any time. The majority of its members were naturally working men, or acknowledged representatives of the working class.... The police, which until then had been the instrument of the Government, was at once stripped of its political attributes, and turned into the responsible, and at all times revocable, agent of the Commune. So were the officials of all other branches of the administration. From the members of the Commune downwards, the public service had to be done at workmen's wages. The privileges and the representation allowances of the high dignitaries of state disappeared along with the high dignitaries themselves.... Having once got rid of the standing army and the police, the instruments of physical force of the old government, the Commune proceeded at once to break the instrument of spiritual suppression, the power of the priests.... The judicial functionaries lost that sham independence... they were thenceforward to be elective, responsible, and revocable."[3]

The Commune, therefore, appears to have replaced the smashed state machine "only" by fuller democracy: abolition of the standing army; all officials to be elected and subject to recall. But as a matter of fact this "only" signifies a gigantic replacement of certain institutions by other institutions of a fundamentally different type. This is exactly a case of "quantity being transformed into quality": democracy, introduced as fully and consistently as is at all conceivable, is transformed from bourgeois into proletarian democracy; from the state (= a special force for the suppression of a particular class) into something which is no longer the state proper.

It is still necessary to suppress the bourgeoisie and crush their resistance. This was particularly necessary for the Commune; and one of the reasons for its defeat was that it did not do this with sufficient determination. The organ of suppression, however, is here the majority of the population, and not a minority, as was always the case under slavery, serfdom, and wage slavery. And since the majority of people itself suppresses its oppressors, a 'special force" for suppression is no longer necessary! In this sense, the state begins to wither away. Instead of the special institutions of a privileged minority (privileged officialdom, the chiefs of the standing army), the majority itself can directly fulfil all these functions, and the more the functions of state power are performed by the people as a whole, the less need there is for the existence of this power.

In this connection, the following measures of the Commune, emphasized by Marx, are particularly noteworthy: the abolition of all representation allowances, and of all monetary privileges to officials, the reduction of the remuneration of all servants of the state to the level of "workmen's wages". This shows more clearly than anything else the turn from bourgeois to proletarian democracy, from the democracy of the oppressors to that of the oppressed classes, from the state as a "special force" for the suppression of a particular class to the suppression of the oppressors by the general force of the majority of the people—the workers and the peasants. And it is on this particularly striking point, perhaps the most important as far as the problem of the state is concerned, that the ideas of Marx have been most completely ignored! In popular commentaries, the number of which is legion, this is not mentioned. The thing done is to keep silent about it as if it were a piece of old-fashioned "naivete", just as Christians, after their religion had been given the status of state religion, "forgot" the "naivete" of primitive Christianity with its democratic revolutionary spirit.

The reduction of the remuneration of high state officials seem "simply" a demand of naive, primitive democracy. One of the "founders" of modern opportunism, the ex-Social-Democrat Eduard Bernstein, has more than once repeated the vulgar bourgeois jeers at "primitive" democracy. Like all opportunists, and like the present Kautskyites, he did not understand at all that, first of all, the transition from capitalism to socialism is impossible without a certain "reversion" to "primitive" democracy (for how else can the majority, and then the whole population without exception, proceed to discharge state functions?); and that, secondly, "primitive democracy" based on capitalism and capitalist culture is not the same as primitive democracy in prehistoric or pre-capitalist times. Capitalist culture has created large-scale production, factories, railways, the postal service, telephones, etc., and on this basis the great majority of the functions of the old "state power" have become so simplified and can be reduced to such exceedingly simple operations of registration, filing, and checking that they can be easily performed by every literate person, can quite easily be performed for ordinary "workmen's wages", and that these functions can (and must) be stripped of every shadow of privilege, of every semblance of "official grandeur".

All officials, without exception, elected and subject to recall at any time, their salaries reduced to the level of ordinary "workmen's wages"—these simple and "self-evident" democratic measures, while completely uniting the interests of the workers and the majority of the peasants, at the same time serve as a bridge leading from capitalism to socialism. These measures concern the reorganization of the state, the purely political reorganization of society; but, of course, they acquire their full meaning and significance only in connection with the "expropriation of the expropriators" either bring accomplished or in preparation, i.e., with the transformation of capitalist private ownership of the means of production into social ownership.

> "The Commune," Marx wrote, "made the catchword of all bourgeois revolutions, cheap government, a reality, by abolishing the two greatest sources of expenditure—the army and the officialdom."

The subordination, however, must be to the armed vanguard of all the exploited and working people, i.e., to the proletariat. A beginning can and must be made at once, overnight, to replace the specific "bossing" of state officials by the simple functions of "foremen and accountants", functions which are already fully within the ability of the average town dweller and can well be performed for "workmen's wages".

We, the workers, shall organize large-scale production on the basis of what capitalism has already created, relying on our own experience as workers, establishing strict, iron discipline backed up by the state power of the armed workers. We shall reduce the role of state officials to that of simply carrying out our instructions as responsible, revocable, modestly paid "foremen and accountants" (of course, with the aid of technicians of all sorts, types and degrees). This is our proletarian task, this is what we can and must start with in accomplishing the proletarian revolution. Such a beginning, on the basis of large-scale production, will of itself lead to the gradual "withering away" of all bureaucracy, to the gradual creation of an order—an order without inverted commas, an order bearing no similarity to wage slavery—an order under which the functions of control and accounting, becoming more and more simple, will be performed by each in turn, will then become a habit and will finally die out as the special functions of a special section of the population.

A witty German Social-Democrat of the seventies of the last century called the postal service an example of the socialist economic system. This is very true. At the present the postal service is a business organized on the lines of state-capitalist monopoly. Imperialism is gradually transforming all trusts into organizations of a similar type, in which, standing over the "common" people, who are overworked and starved, one has the same bourgeois bureaucracy. But the mechanism of social management is here already to hand. Once we have overthrown the capitalists, crushed the resistance of these exploiters with the iron hand of the armed workers, and smashed the bureaucratic machinery of the modern state, we shall have a splendidly-equipped mechanism, freed from the "parasite", a mechanism which can very well be set going by the united workers themselves, who will hire technicians, foremen and accountants, and pay them all, as indeed all "state" officials in general, workmen's wages. Here is a concrete, practical task which can immediately be fulfilled in relation to all trusts, a task whose fulfilment will rid the working people of exploitation, a task which takes account of what the Commune had already begun to practice (particularly in building up the state).

To organize the whole economy on the lines of the postal service so that the technicians, foremen and accountants, as well as all officials, shall receive salaries no higher than "a workman's wage", all under the control and leadership of the armed proletariat—that is our immediate aim. This is what will bring about the abolition of parliamentarism and the preservation of representative institutions. This is what will rid the laboring classes of the bourgeoisie's prostitution of these institutions.

4. ORGANISATION OF NATIONAL UNITY

"In a brief sketch of national organization which the Commune had no time to develop, it states explicitly that the Commune was to be the political form of even the smallest village...." The communes were to elect the "National Delegation" in Paris.

"... The few but important functions which would still remain for a central government were not to to be suppressed, as had been deliberately mis-stated, but were to be transferred to communal, i.e., strictly responsible, officials.

"... National unity was not to be broken, but, on the contrary, organized by the communal constitution; it was to become a reality by the destruction of state power which posed as the embodiment of that unity yet wanted to be independent of, and superior to, the nation, on whose body it was but a parasitic excrescence. While the merely repressive organs of the old governmental power were to be amputated, its legitimate functions were to be wrested from an authority claiming the right to stand above society, and restored to the responsible servants of society."

The extent to which the opportunists of present-day Social-Democracy have failed—perhaps it would be more true to say, have refused—to understand these observations of Marx is best shown by that book of Herostratean fame of the renegade Bernstein, *The Premises of Socialism and the Tasks of the Social-Democrats*. It is in connection with the above passage from Marx that Bernstein wrote that "as far as its political content", this programme "displays, in all its essential features, the greatest similarity to the federalism of Proudhon.... In spite of all the other points of difference between Marx and the 'petty-bourgeois' Proudhon [Bernstein places the word "petty-bourgeois" in inverted commas, to make it sound ironical] on these points, their lines of reasoning run as close as could be." Of course, Bernstein continues, the importance of the municipalities is growing, but "it seems doubtful to me whether the first job of democracy would be such a dissolution [Auflosung] of the modern states and such a complete transformation [Umwandlung] of their organization as is visualized by Marx and Proudhon (the formation of a National Assembly from delegates of the provincial of district assemblies, which, in their turn, would consist of delegates from the communes), so that consequently the previous mode of national representation would disappear." (Bernstein, *Premises*, German edition, 1899, pp.134 and 136)

To confuse Marx's view on the "destruction of state power, a parasitic excrescence", with Proudhon's federalism is positively monstrous! But it is no accident, for it never occurs to the opportunist that Marx does not speak here at all about federalism as opposed to centralism, but about smashing the old, bourgeois state machine which exists in all bourgeois countries.

The only thing that does occur to the opportunist is what he sees around him, in an environment of petty-bourgeois philistinism and "reformists" stagnation, namely, only "municipalities"! The opportunist has even grown out of the habit of thinking about proletarian revolution.

It is ridiculous. But the remarkable thing is that nobody argued with Bernstein on this point. Bernstein has been refuted by many, especially by Plekhanov in Russian literature and by Kautsky in European literature, but neither of them has said anything about this distortion of Marx by Bernstein.

The opportunist has so much forgotten how to think in a revolutionary way and to dwell on revolution that he attributes "federalism" to Marx, whom he confuses with the founder of anarchism, Proudhon. As for Kautsky and Plekhanov, who claim to be orthodox Marxists and defenders of the theory of revolutionary Marxism, they are silent on this point! Here is one of the roots of the extreme vulgarization of the views on the difference between Marxism and anarchism, which is characteristic of both the Kautskyites and the opportunists, and which we shall discuss again later.

There is not a trace of federalism in Marx's above-quoted observation on the experience of the Commune. Marx agreed with Proudhon on the very point that the opportunist Bernstein did not see. Marx disagreed with Proudhon on the very point on which Bernstein found a similarity between them.

Marx agreed with Proudhon in that they both stood for the "smashing" of the modern state machine. Neither the opportunists nor the Kautskyites wish to see the similarity of views on this point between Marxism and anarchism (both Proudhon and Bakunin) because this is where they have departed from Marxism.

Marx disagreed both with Proudhon and Bakunin precisely on the question of federalism (not to mention the dictatorship of the proletariat). Federalism as a principle follows logically from the petty-bourgeois views of anarchism. Marx was a centralist. There is no departure whatever from centralism in his observations just quoted. Only those who are imbued with the philistine "superstitious belief" in the state can mistake the destruction of the bourgeois state machine for the destruction of centralism!

Now if the proletariat and the poor peasants take state power into their own hands, organize themselves quite freely in communes, and unite the action of all the communes in striking at capital, in crushing the resistance of the capitalists, and in transferring the privately-owned railways, factories, land and so on to the entire nation, to the whole of society, won't that be centralism? Won't that be the most consistent democratic centralism and, moreover, proletarian centralism?

Bernstein simply cannot conceive of the possibility of voluntary centralism, of the voluntary fusion of the proletarian communes, for the sole purpose of destroying bourgeois rule and the bourgeois state machine. Like all philistines, Bernstein pictures centralism as something which can be imposed and maintained solely from above, and solely by the bureaucracy and military clique.

As though foreseeing that his views might be distorted, Marx expressly emphasized that the charge that the Commune had wanted to destroy national unity, to abolish the central authority, was a deliberate fraud. Marx purposely used the words: "National unity was... to be organized", so as to oppose conscious, democratic, proletarian centralism to bourgeois, military, bureaucratic centralism.

But there are none so deaf as those who will not hear. And the very thing the opportunists of present-day Social-Democracy do not want to hear about it the destruction of state power, the amputation of the parasitic excrescence.

5. ABOLITION OF THE PARASITE STATE

We have already quoted Marx's words on the subject, and we must now supplement them.

"It is generally the fate of new historical creations," he wrote, "to be mistaken for the counterpart of older and even defunct forms of social life, to which they may bear a certain likeness. Thus, this new Commune, which breaks [bricht, smashes] the modern state power, has been regarded as a revival of the medieval communes... as a federation of small states (as Montesquieu and the Girondins[4] visualized it)... as an exaggerated form of the old struggle against overcentralization....

"... The Communal Constitution would have restored to the social body all the forces hitherto absorbed by that parasitic excrescence, the 'state', feeding upon and hampering the free movement of society. By this one act it would have initiated the regeneration of France....

"... The Communal Constitution would have brought the rural producers under the intellectual lead of the central towns of their districts, and there secured to them, in the town working men, the natural trustees of their interests. The very existence of the Commune involved, as a matter of course, local self-government, but no longer as a counterpoise to state power, now become superfluous."

"Breaking state power", which as a "parasitic excrescence"; its "amputation", its "smashing"; "state power, now become superfluous"—these are the expressions Marx used in regard to the state when appraising and analyzing the experience of the Commune.

All this was written a little less than half a century ago; and now one has to engage in excavations, as it were, in order to bring undistorted Marxism to the knowledge of the mass of the people. The conclusions drawn from the observation of the last great revolution which Marx lived through were forgotten just when the time for the next great proletarian revolution has arrived.

"... The multiplicity of interpretations to which the Commune has been subjected, and the multiplicity of interests which expressed themselves in it show that it was a thoroughly flexible political form, while all previous forms of government had been essentially repressive. Its true secret was this: it was essentially a working-class government, the result of the struggle of the producing against the appropriating class, the political form at last discovered under which the economic emancipation of labor could be accomplished....

"Except on this last condition, the Communal Constitution would have been an impossibility and a delusion...."

The utopians busied themselves with "discovering" political forms under which the socialist transformation of society was to take place. The anarchists dismissed the question of political forms altogether. The opportunists of present-day Social-Democracy accepted the bourgeois political forms of the parliamentary democratic state as the limit which should not be overstepped; they battered their foreheads praying before this "model", and denounced as anarchism every desire to break these forms.

Marx deduced from the whole history of socialism and the political struggle that the state was bound to disappear, and that the transitional form of its disappearance (the transition from state to non-state) would be the "proletariat organized as the ruling class". Marx, however, did not set out to discover the political forms of this future stage. He limited himself to carefully observing French history, to analyzing it, and to drawing the conclusion to which the year 1851 had led, namely, that matters were moving towards destruction of the bourgeois state machine.

And when the mass revolutionary movement of the proletariat burst forth, Marx, in spite of its failure, in spite of its short life and patent weakness, began to study the forms it had discovered.

The Commune is the form "at last discovered" by the proletarian revolution, under which the economic emancipation of labor can take place.

The Commune is the first attempt by a proletarian revolution to smash the bourgeois state machine; and it is the political form "at last discovered", by which the smashed state machine can and must be replaced.

We shall see further on that the Russian revolutions of 1905 and 1917, in different circumstances and under different conditions, continue the work of the Commune and confirm Marx's brilliant historical analysis. □

Chapter 4

Supplementary explanations by Engels

MARX gave the fundamentals concerning the significance of the experience of the Commune. Engels returned to the same subject time and again, and explained Marx's analysis and conclusions, sometimes elucidating other aspects of the question with such power and vividness that it is necessary to deal with his explanations specially.

1. THE HOUSING QUESTION

In his work, *The Housing Question* (1872), Engels already took into account the experience of the Commune, and dealt several times with the tasks of the revolution in relation to the state. It is interesting to note that the treatment of this specific subject clearly revealed, on the one hand, points of similarity between the proletarian state and the present state—points that warrant speaking of the state in both cases—and, on the other hand, points of difference between them, or the transition to the destruction of the state.

"How is the housing question to be settled then? In present-day society, it is settled just as any other social question: by the gradual economic levelling of demand and supply, a settlement which reproduces the question itself again and again and therefore is no settlement. How a social revolution would settle this question not only depends on the circumstances in each particular case, but is also connected with much more far-reaching questions, one of the most fundamental of which is the abolition of the antithesis between town and country. As it is not our task to create utopian systems for the organization of the future society, it would be more than idle to go into the question here. But one thing is certain: there is already a sufficient quantity of houses in the big cities to remedy immediately all real 'housing shortage', provided they are used judiciously. This can naturally only occur through the expropriation of the present owners and by quartering in their houses homeless workers or workers overcrowded in their present homes. As soon as the proletariat has won political power, such a measure prompted by concern for the common good will be just as easy to carry out as are other expropriations and billetings by the present-day state." (German edition, 1887, p. 22)[1]

The change in the form of state power is not examined here, but only the content of its activity. Expropriations and billetings take place by order even of the present state. From the formal point of view, the proletarian state will also "order" the occupation of dwellings and expropriation of houses. But it is clear that the old executive apparatus, the bureaucracy, which is connected with the bourgeoisie, would simply be unfit to carry out the orders of the proletarian state.

"... It must be pointed out that the 'actual seizure' of all the instruments of labor, the taking possession of industry as a whole by the working people, is the exact opposite of the Proudhonist 'redemption'. In the latter case the individual worker becomes the owner of the dwelling, the peasant farm, the instruments of labor; in the former case, the 'working people' remain the collective owners of the houses, factories and instruments of labor, and will hardly permit their use, at least during a transitional period, by individuals or associations without compensation for the cost. In the same way, the abolition of property in land is not the abolition of ground rent but its transfer, if in a modified form, to society. The actual seizure of all the instruments of labor by the working people, therefore, does not at all preclude the retention of rent relations." (p.68)

We shall examine the question touched upon in this passage, namely, the economic basis for the withering away of the state, in the next chapter. Engels expresses himself most cautiously. saying that the proletarian state would "hardly" permit the use of houses without payment, "at least during a transitional period". The letting of houses owed by the whole people to individual families presupposes the collection of rent, a certain amount of control, and the employment of some standard in allotting the housing. All this calls for a certain form of state, but it does not at all call for a special military bureaucratic apparatus, with officials occupying especially privileged positions. The transition to a situation in which it will be possible to supply dwellings rent-free depends on the complete "withering away" of the state.

Speaking of the Blanquists' adoption of the fundamental position of Marxism after the Commune and under the influence of its experience, Engels, in passing, formulates this position as follows:

> "... Necessity of political action by the proletariat and of its dictatorship as the transition to the abolition of classes and, with them, of the state...." (p.55)

Addicts of hair-splitting criticism, or bourgeois "exterminators of Marxism", will perhaps see a contradiction between this recognition of the "abolition of the state" and repudiation of this formula as an anarchist one in the above passage from *Anti-Dühring*. It would not be surprising if the opportunists classed Engels, too, as an "anarchist", for it is becoming increasingly common with the social-chauvinists to accuse the internationalists of anarchism.

Marxism has always taught that with the abolition of classes the state will also be abolished. The well-known passage on the "withering away of the state in *Anti-Dühring* accuses the anarchists not simply of favoring the abolition of the state, but of preaching that the state can be abolished "overnight".

As the now prevailing "Social-Democratic" doctrine completely distorts the relation of Marxism to anarchism on the question of the abolition of the state, it will be particularly useful to recall a certain controversy in which Marx and Engels came out against the anarchists.

CONTROVERSY WITH THE ANARCHISTS

This controversy took place in 1873. Marx and Engels contributed articles against the Proudhonists, "autonomists" or "anti- authoritarians", to an Italian socialist annual, and it was not until 1913 that these articles appeared in German in *Neue Zeit*.[2]

> "If the political struggle of the working class assumes revolutionary form," wrote Marx, ridiculing the anarchists for their repudiation of politics, "and if the workers set up their revolutionary dictatorship in place of the dictatorship of the bourgeoisie, they commit the terrible crime of violating principles, for in order to satisfy their wretched, vulgar everyday needs and to crush the resistance of the bourgeoisie, they give the state a revolutionary and transient form, instead of laying down their arms and abolishing the state." (*Neue Zeit* Vol.XXXII, 1, 1913-14, p.40)

It was solely against this kind of "abolition" of the state that Marx fought in refuting the anarchists! He did not at all oppose the view that the state would disappear when classes disappeared, or that it would be abolished when classes were abolished. What he did oppose was the proposition that the workers should renounce the use of arms, organized violence, that is, the state, which is to serve to "crush the resistance of the bourgeoisie".

To prevent the true meaning of his struggle against anarchism from being distorted, Marx expressly emphasized the "revolutionary and transient form" of the state which the proletariat needs. The proletariat needs the state only temporarily. We do not after all differ with the anarchists on the question of the abolition of the state as the aim. We maintain that, to achieve this aim, we must temporarily make use of the instruments, resources, and methods of state power against the exploiters, just as the temporary dictatorship of the oppressed class is necessary for the abolition of classes. Marx chooses the sharpest and clearest way of stating his case against the anarchists: After overthrowing the yoke of the capitalists, should the workers "lay down their arms", or use them against the capitalists in order to crush their resistance? But what is the systematic use of arms by one class against another if not a "transient form" of state?

Let every Social-Democrat ask himself: Is that how he has been posing the question of the state in controversy with the anarchists? Is that how it has been posed by the vast majority of the official socialist parties of the Second International?

Engels expounds the same ideas in much greater detail and still more popularly. First of all he ridicules the muddled ideas of the Proudhonists, who call themselves "anti-authoritarians", i.e., repudiated all authority, all subordination, all power. Take a factory, a railway, a ship on the high seas, said Engels: is it not clear that not one of these complex technical establishments, based on the use of machinery and the systematic co-operation of many people, could function without a certain amount of subordination and, conse-quently, without a certain amount of authority or power?

> "... When I counter the most rabid anti-authoritari-ans with these arguments, they only answer they can give me is the following: Oh, that's true, except that here it is not a question of authority with which we vest our del-egates, but of a commission! These people imagine they can change a thing by changing its name...."

Having thus shown that authority and autonomy are relative terms, that the sphere of their application varies with the various phases of social development, that it is absurd to take them as abso-lutes, and adding that the sphere of application of machinery and large-scale production is steadily expanding, Engels passes from the general discussion of authority to the question of the state.

> "Had the autonomists," he wrote, "contented them-selves with saying that the social organization of the future would allow authority only within the bounds which the conditions of production make inevitable, one could have come to terms with them. But they are blind to all facts that make authority necessary and they passion-ately fight the word.

"Why do the anti-authoritarians not confine themselves to crying out against political authority, the state?
All socialists are agreed that the state, and with it political
authority, will disappear as a result of the coming social
revolution, that is, that public functions will lose their
political character and become mere administrative functions of watching over social interests. But the anti-authoritarians demand that the political state be abolished at
one stroke, even before the social relations that gave both
to it have been destroyed. They demand that the first act
of the social revolution shall be the abolition of authority.

"Have these gentlemen ever seen a revolution? A
revolution is certainly the most authoritarian thing there
is; it is an act whereby one part of the population imposes
its will upon the other part by means of rifles, bayonets
and cannon, all of which are highly authoritarian means.
And the victorious party must maintain its rule by means
of the terror which its arms inspire in the reactionaries.
Would the Paris Commune have lasted more than a day if
it had not used the authority of the armed people against
the bourgeoisie? Cannot we, on the contrary, blame it for
having made too little use of that authority? Therefore,
one of two things: either that anti-authoritarians don't
know what they are talking about, in which case they are
creating nothing but confusion. Or they do know, and in
that case they are betraying the cause of the proletariat. In
either case they serve only reaction." (p.39)

This argument touches upon questions which should be
examined in connection with the relationship between politics and
economics during the withering away of the state (the next chapter
is devoted to this). These questions are: the transformation of public
functions from political into simple functions of administration, and
the "political state". This last term, one particularly liable to misun-
derstanding, indicates the process of the withering away of the state:
at a certain stage of this process, the state which is withering away
may be called a non-political state.

Against, the most remarkable thing in this argument of Engels' is the way he states his case against the anarchists. Social-Democrats, claiming to be disciples of Engels, have argued on this subject against the anarchists millions of times since 1873, but they have not argued as Marxists could and should. The anarchist idea of abolition of the state is muddled and non-revolutionary—that is how Engels put it. It is precisely the revolution in its rise and development, with its specific tasks in relation to violence, authority, power, the state, that the anarchists refuse to see.

The usual criticism of anarchism by present-day Social-Democrats has boiled down to the purest philistine banality: "We recognize the state, whereas the anarchists do not!" Naturally, such banality cannot but repel workers who are at all capable of thinking and revolutionary-minded. What Engels says is different. He stresses that all socialists recognize that the state will disappear as a result of the socialist revolution. He then deals specifically with the question of the revolution—the very question which, as a rule, the Social-Democrats evade out of opportunism, leaving it, so to speak, exclusively for the anarchists "to work out". And when dealing with this question, Engels takes the bull by the horns; he asks: should not the Commune have made more use of the revolutionary power of the state, that is, of the proletariat armed and organized as the ruling class?

Prevailing official Social-Democracy usually dismissed the question of the concrete tasks of the proletariat in the revolution either with a philistine sneer, or, at best, with the sophistic evasion: "The future will show". And the anarchists were justified in saying about such Social-Democrats that they were failing in their task of giving the workers a revolutionary education. Engels draws upon the experience of the last proletarian revolution precisely for the purpose of making a most concrete study of what should be done by the proletariat, and in what manner, in relation to both the banks and the state.

LETTER TO BEBEL

One of the most, if not the most, remarkable observation on the state in the works of Marx and Engels is contained in the following passage in Engels' letter to Bebel dated March 18-28, 1875. This letter, we may observe in parenthesis, was, as far as we know, first published by Bebel in the second volume of his memoirs (*Aus meinem*

Leben), which appeared in 1911, i.e., 36 years after the letter had been written and sent.

Engels wrote to Bebel criticizing the same draft of the Gotha Programme which Marx criticized in his famous letter to Bracke. Referring specially to the question of the state, Engels said:

> "The free people's state has been transferred into the free state. Taken in its grammatical sense, a free state is one where the state is free in relation to its citizens, hence a state with a despotic government. The whole talk about the state should be dropped, especially since the Commune, which was no longer a state in the proper sense of the word. The 'people's state' has been thrown in our faces by the anarchists to the point of disgust, although already Marx's book against Proudhon and later the *Communist Manifesto* say plainly that with the introduction of the socialist order of society the state dissolves of itself [sich auflost] and disappears. As the state is only a transitional institution which is used in the struggle, in the revolution, to hold down one's adversaries by force, it is sheer nonsense to talk of a 'free people's state'; so long as the proletariat still needs the state, it does not need it in the interests of freedom but in order to hold down its adversaries, and as soon as it becomes possible to speak of freedom the state as such ceases to exist. We would therefore propose replacing the state everywhere by *Gemeinwesen*, a good old German word which can very well take the place of the French word commune." (pp.321-22 of the German original.)[3]

It should be borne in mind that this letter refers to the party programme which Marx criticized in a letter dated only a few weeks later than the above (Marx's letter is dated May 5, 1875), and that at the time Engels was living with Marx in London. Consequently, when he says "we" in the last sentence, Engels undoubtedly, in his own as well as in Marx's name, suggests to the leader of the German workers' party that the word "state" be struck out of the programme and replaced by the word "community".

What a howl about "anarchism" would be raised by the leading lights of present-day "Marxism", which has been falsified for the convenience of the opportunists, if such an amendment of the programme were suggested to them!

Let them howl. This will earn them the praises of the bourgeoisie.

And we shall go on with our work. In revising the programme of our Party, we must by all means take the advice of Engels and Marx into consideration in order to come nearer the truth, to restore Marxism by ridding it of distortions, to guide the struggle of the working class for its emancipation more correctly. Certainly no one opposed to the advice of Engels and Marx will be found among the Bolsheviks. The only difficulty that may perhaps arise will be in regard to the term. In German there are two words meaning "community", of which Engels used the one which does not denote a single community, but their totality, a system of communities. In Russian there is no such word, and we may have to choose the French word "commune", although this also has its drawbacks.

"The Commune was no longer a state in the proper sense of the word"—this is the most theoretically important statement Engels makes. After what has been said above, this statement is perfectly clear. The Commune was ceasing to be a state since it had to suppress, not the majority of the population, but a minority (the exploiters). It had smashed the bourgeois state machine. In place of a special coercive force the population itself came on the scene. All this was a departure from the state in the proper sense of the word. And had the Commune become firmly established, all traces of the state in it would have "withered away" of themselves; it would not have had to "abolish" the institutions of the state—they would have ceased to function as they ceased to have anything to do.

"The 'people's state' has been thrown in our faces by the anarchists". In saying this, Engels above all has in mind Bakunin and his attacks on the German Social-Democrats. Engels admits that these attacks were justified insofar as the "people's state" was as much an absurdity and as much a departure from socialism as the "free people's state". Engels tried to put the struggle of the German Social-Democrats against the anarchists on the right lines, to make this struggle correct in principle, to ride it of opportunist prejudices concerning the "state". Unfortunately, Engels' letter was pigeon-holed for 36 years. We shall see farther on that, even after this letter was published, Kautsky persisted in virtually the same mistakes against which Engels had warned.

Bebel replied to Engels in a letter dated September 21, 1875, in which he wrote, among other things, that he "fully agreed" with Engels' opinion of the draft programme, and that he had reproached Liebknecht with readiness to make concessions (p.334 of the German edition of Bebel's memoirs, Vol.II). But if we take Bebel's pamphlet, *Our Aims*, we find there views on the state that are absolutely wrong.

"The state must... be transformed from one based on class rule into a people's state." (*Unsere Ziele*, 1886, p.14)

This was printed in the ninth (ninth!) edition of Bebel's pamphlet! It is not surprising that opportunist views on the state, so persistently repeated, were absorbed by the German Social-Democrats, especially as Engels' revolutionary interpretations had been safely pigeon-holed, and all the conditions of life were such as to "wean" them from revolution for a long time.

2. CRITICISM OF THE DRAFT OF THE ERFURT PROGRAMME

In analyzing Marxist teachings on the state, the criticism of the draft of the Erfurt Programme,[4] sent by Engels to Kautsky on June 29, 1891, and published only 10 years later in *Neue Zeit*, cannot be ignored; for it is with the opportunist views of the Social-Democrats on questions of state organization that this criticism is mainly concerned.

We shall note in passing that Engels also makes an exceedingly valuable observation on economic questions, which shows how attentively and thoughtfully he watched the various changes occurring in modern capitalism, and how for this reason he was able to foresee to a certain extent the tasks of our present, the imperialist, epoch. Here is that observation: referring to the word "planlessness" (Planlosigkeit), used in the draft programme, as characteristic of capitalism, Engels wrote:

"When we pass from joint-stock companies to trusts which assume control over, and monopolize, whole industries, it is not only private production that ceases, but also planlessness." (*Neue Zeit*, Vol. XX, 1, 1901-02, p.8)

Here we have what is most essential in the theoretical appraisal of the latest phase of capitalism, i.e., imperialism, namely, that capitalism becomes monopoly capitalism. The latter must be emphasized because the erroneous bourgeois reformist assertion that monopoly capitalism or state-monopoly capitalism is no longer capitalism, but can now be called "state socialism" and so on, is very common. The trusts, of course, never provided, do not now provide, and cannot provide complete planning. But however much they do plan, however much the capitalist magnates calculate in advance the volume of production on a national and even on an international scale, and however much they systematically regulate it, we still remain under capitalism—at its new stage, it is true, but still capitalism, without a doubt. The "proximity" of such capitalism to socialism should serve genuine representatives of the proletariat as an argument proving the proximity, facility, feasibility, and urgency of the socialist revolution, and not at all as an argument for tolerating the repudiation of such a revolution and the efforts to make capitalism look more attractive, something which all reformists are trying to do.

But to return to the question of the state. In his letter Engels makes three particularly valuable suggestions: first, in regard to the republic; second, in regard to the connection between the national question and state organization; and, third, in regard to local self-government.

In regard to the republic, Engels made this the focal point of this criticism of the draft of the Erfurt Programme. And when we recall the importance which the Erfurt Programme acquired for all the Social- Democrats of the world, and that it became the model for the whole Second International, we may say without exaggeration that Engels thereby criticizes the opportunism of the whole Second International.

"The political demands of the draft," Engels wrote, "have one great fault. It lacks [Engels' italics] precisely what should have been said."

And, later on, he makes it clear that the German Constitution is, strictly speaking, a copy of the extremely reactionary Constitution of 1850, that the Reichstag is only, as Wilhelm Liebknecht put it, "the fig leaf of absolutism" and that to wish "to transform all the instruments of labor into common property" on the basis of a constitution which legalizes the existence of petty states and the federation of petty German states is an "obvious absurdity".

"To touch on that is dangerous, however," Engels added, knowing only too well that it was impossible legally to include in the programme the demand for a republic in Germany. But he refused to merely accept this obvious consideration which satisfied "everybody". He continued: "Nevertheless, somehow or other, the thing has to be attacked. How necessary this is is shown precisely at the present time by opportunism, which is gaining ground [einreissende] in a large section of the Social-Democrat press. Fearing a renewal of the Anti-Socialist Law,[5] or recalling all manner of overhasty pronouncements made during the reign of that law, they now want the Party to find the present legal order in Germany adequate for putting through all Party demands by peaceful means...."

Engels particularly stressed the fundamental fact that the German Social-Democrats were prompted by fear of a renewal of the Anti- Socialist Law, and explicitly described it as opportunism; he declared that precisely because there was no republic and no freedom in Germany, the dreams of a "peaceful" path were perfectly absurd. Engels was careful not to tie his hands. He admitted that in republican or very free countries "one can conceive" (only "conceive"!) of a peaceful development towards socialism, but in Germany, he repeated,

"... in Germany, where the government is almost omnipotent and the Reichstag and all other representative bodies have no real power, to advocate such a thing in Germany, where, moreover, there is no need to do so, means removing the fig leaf from absolutism and becoming oneself a screen for its nakedness."

The great majority of the official leaders of the German Social-Democratic Party, which pigeon-holed this advice, have really proved to be a screen for absolutism.

"... In the long run such a policy can only lead one's own party astray. They push general, abstract political questions into the foreground, thereby concealing the immediate concrete questions, which at the moment of the first great events, the first political crisis, automatically pose themselves. What can result from this except that at the decisive moment the party suddenly proves helpless and that uncertainty and discord on the most decisive issues reign in it because these issues have never been discussed? ...

"This forgetting of the great, the principal considerations for the momentary interests of the day, this struggling and striving for the success of the moment regardless of later consequences, this sacrifice of the future of the movement for its present may be 'honestly' meant, but it is and remains opportunism, and 'honest' opportunism is perhaps the most dangerous of all....

"If one thing is certain it is that our party and the working class can only come to power in the form of the democratic republic. This is even the specific form for the dictatorship of the proletariat, as the Great French Revolution has already shown...."

Engels realized here in a particularly striking form the fundamental idea which runs through all of Marx's works, namely, that the democratic republic is the nearest approach to the dictatorship of the proletariat. For such a republic, without in the least abolishing the rule of capital, and, therefore, the oppression of the masses and the class struggle, inevitably leads to such an extension, development, unfolding, and intensification of this struggle that, as soon as it becomes possible to meet the fundamental interests of the oppressed masses, this possibility is realized inevitably and solely through the dictatorship of the proletariat, through the leadership of those masses by the proletariat. These, too, are "forgotten words" of Marxism for the whole of the Second International, and the fact that they have been forgotten was demonstrated with particular vividness by the history of the Menshevik Party during the first six months of the Russian revolution of 1917.

On the subject of a federal republic, in connection with the national composition of the population, Engels wrote:

> "What should take the place of the present-day Germany [with its reactionary monarchical Constitution and its equally reactionary division into petty states, a division which perpetuates all the specific features of "Prussianism" instead of dissolving them in Germany as a whole]? In my view, the proletariat can only use the form of the one and indivisible republic. In the gigantic territory of the United States, a federal republic is still, on the whole, a necessity, although in the Eastern states it is already becoming a hindrance. It would be a step forward in Britain where the two islands are peopled by four nations and in spite of a single Parliament three different systems of legislation already exist side by side. In little Switzerland, it has long been a hindrance, tolerable only because Switzerland is content to be a purely passive member of the European state system. For Germany, federalization on the Swiss model would be an enormous step backward. Two points distinguish a union state from a completely unified state: first, that each member state, each canton, has its own civil and criminal legislative and judicial system, and, second, that alongside a popular chamber there is also a federal chamber in which each canton, whether large or small, votes as such." In Germany, the union state is the transition to the completely unified state, and the "revolution from above" of 1866 and 1870 must not be reversed but supplemented by a "movement from below".

Far from being indifferent to the forms of state, Engels, on the contrary, tried to analyze the transitional forms with the utmost thoroughness in order to establish, in accordance with the concrete historical peculiarities of each particular case, from what and to what the given transitional form is passing.

Approaching the matter from the standpoint of the proletariat and the proletarian revolution, Engels, like Marx, upheld democratic centralism, the republic—one and indivisible. He regarded the federal republic either as an exception and a hindrance to development, or as a transition from a monarchy to a centralized republic, as a "step forward" under certain special conditions. And among these special conditions, he puts the national question to the fore.

Although mercilessly criticizing the reactionary nature of small states, and the screening of this by the national question in certain concrete cases, Engels, like Marx, never betrayed the slightest desire to brush aside the national question—a desire of which the Dutch and Polish Marxists, who proceed from their perfectly justified opposition to the narrow philistine nationalism of "their" little states, are often guilty.

Even in regard to Britain, where geographical conditions, a common language and the history of many centuries would seem to have "put an end" to the national question in the various small divisions of the country—even in regard to that country, Engels reckoned with the plain fact that the national question was not yet a thing of the past, and recognized in consequence that the establishment of a federal republic would be a "step forward". Of course, there is not the slightest hint here of Engels abandoning the criticism of the shortcomings of a federal republic or renouncing the most determined advocacy of, and struggle for, a unified and centralized democratic republic.

But Engels did not at all mean democratic centralism in the bureaucratic sense in which the term is used by bourgeois and petty-bourgeois ideologists, the anarchists among the latter. His idea of centralism did not in the least preclude such broad local self-government as would combine the voluntary defence of the unity of the state by the "communes" and districts, and the complete elimination of all bureaucratic practices and all "ordering" from above. Carrying forward the programme views of Marxism on the state, Engels wrote:

"So, then, a unified republic—but not in the sense
of the present French Republic, which is nothing but the
Empire established in 1798 without the Emperor. From
1792 to 1798 each French department, each commune
[Gemeinde], enjoyed complete self-government on the
American model, and this is what we too must have. How
self-government is to be organized and how we can manage,
without a bureaucracy has been shown to us by America
and the first French Republic, and is being shown even
today by Australia, Canada and the other English colonies.
And a provincial [regional] and communal self-government
of this type is far freer than, for instance, Swiss federalism,
under which, it is true, the canton is very independent in
relation to the Bund [i.e., the federated state as a whole],
but is also independent in relation to the district [Bezirk]
and the commune. The cantonal governments appoint the
district governors [Bezirksstatthalter] and prefects—which
is unknown in English-speaking countries and which we
want to abolish here as resolutely in the future as the
Prussian Landrate and Regierungsrate" (commissioners,
district police chiefs, governors, and in general all officials
appointed from above). Accordingly, Engels proposes the
following words for the self-government clause in the
programme: "Complete self-government for the provinces
[gubernias or regions], districts and communes through
officials elected by universal suffrage. The abolition of all
local and provincial authorities appointed by the state."

I have already had occassion to point out—in *Pravda* (No.68,
May 28, 1917), which was suppressed by the government of Kerensky
and other "socialist" Ministers—how on this point (of course, not on
this point alone by any mens) our pseudo-socialist representatives of
pseudo-revolutionary pseudo-democracy have made glaring departures
from democracy. Naturally, people who have bound themselves by a
"coalition" to the imperialist bourgeoisie have remained deaf to this
criticism.

It is extremely important to note that Engels, armed with facts,
disproved by a most precise example the prejudice which is very

widespread, particularly among petty-bourgeois democrats, that a federal republic necessarily means a greater amount of freedom than a centralized republic. This is wrong. It is disproved by the facts cited by Engels regarding the centralized French Republic of 1792-98 and the federal Swiss Republic. The really democratic centralized republic gave more freedom that the federal republic. In other words, the greatest amount of local, regional, and other freedom known in history was accorded by a centralized and not a federal republic.

Insufficient attention has been and is being paid in our Party propaganda and agitation to this fact, as, indeed, to the whole question of the federal and the centralized republic and local self-government.

THE 1891 PREFACE TO MARX'S "THE CIVIL WAR IN FRANCE"

In his preface to the third edition of *The Civil War in France* (this preface is dated March 18, 1891, and was originally published in *Neue Zeit*), Engels, in addition to some interesting incidental remarks on questions concerning the attitude towards the state, gave a remarkably vivid summary of the lessons of the Commune.[6] This summary, made more profound by the entire experience of the 20 years that separated the author from the Commune, and directed expressly against the "superstitious belief in the state" so widespread in Germany, may justly be called the last word of Marxism on the question under consideration.

In France, Engels observed, the workers emerged with arms from every revolution: "therefore the disarming of the workers was the first commandment for the bourgeois, who were at the helm of the state. Hence, after every revolution won by the workers, a new struggle, ending with the defeat of the workers."

This summary of the experience of bourgeois revolutions is as concise as it is expressive. The essence of the matter—among other things, on the question of the state (has the oppressed class arms?)—is here remarkably well-grasped. It is precisely this essence that is most often evaded by both professors influenced by bourgeois ideology, and by petty-bourgeois democrats. In the Russian revolution of 1917, the honor (Cavaignac honor) of blabbing this secret of bourgeois revolutions fell to the Menshevik, would-be Marxist, Tsereteli. In his "historic" speech of June 11, Tsereteli blurted out that the bourgeoisie were determined to disarm the Petrograd workers—presenting, of course, this decision as his own, and as a necessity for the "state" in general!

Tsereteli's historical speech of June 11 will, of course, serve every historian of the revolution of 1917 as a graphic illustration of how the Social-Revolutionary and Menshevik bloc, led by Mr. Tsereteli, deserted to the bourgeoisie against the revolutionary proletariat.

Another incidental remark of Engels', also connected with the question of the state, deals with religion. It is well-known that the German Social-Democrats, as they degenerated and became increasingly opportunist, slipped more and more frequently into the philistine misinterpretation of the celebrated formula: "Religion is to be declared a private matter." That is, the formula was twisted to mean that religion was a private matter even for the party of the revolutionary proletariat!! It was against this complete betrayal of the revolutionary programme of the proletariat that Engels vigorously protested. In 1891 he saw only the very feeble beginnings of opportunism in his party, and, therefore, he expressed himself with extreme caution:

> "As almost only workers, or recognized representatives of the workers, sat in the Commune, its decisions bore a decidedly proletarian character. Either they decreed reforms which the republican bourgeoisie had failed to pass solely out of cowardice, but which provided a necessary basis for the free activity of the working class—such as the realization of the principle that *in relation to the state* religion is a purely private matter—or the Commune promulgated decrees which were in the direct interest of the working class and in part cut deeply into the old order of society."

Engels deliberately emphasized the words "in relation to the state" as a straight thrust at at German opportunism, which had declared religion to be a private matter in relation to the party, thus degrading the party of the revolutionary proletariat to the level of the most vulgar "free- thinking" philistinism, which is prepared to allow a non-denominational status, but which renounces the party struggle against the opium of religion which stupifies the people.

The future historian of the German Social-Democrats, in tracing the roots of their shameful bankruptcy in 1914, will find a fair amount of interesting material on this question, beginning with the evasive declarations in the articles of the party's ideological leader, Kautsky, which throw the door wide open to opportunism, and ending with the attitude of the party towards the "Los-von-Kirche-Bewegung"[7] (the "Leave-the-Church" movement) in 1913.

But let us see how, 20 years after the Commune, Engels summed up its lessons for the fighting proletariat.

Here are the lessons to which Engels attached prime importance:

"... It was precisely the oppressing power of the former centralized government, army, political parties, bureaucracy, which Napoleon had created in 1798 and which every new government had since then taken over as a welcome instrument and used against its opponents—it was this power which was to fall everywhere, just as it had fallen in Paris.

"From the very outset the Commune had to recognize that the working class, once in power, could not go on managing with the old state machine; that in order not to lose again its only just-gained supremacy, this working class must, on the one hand, do away with all the old machinery of oppression previously used against it itself, and, on the other, safeguard itself against its own deputies and officials, by declaring them all, without exception, subject to recall at any time...."

Engels emphasized once again that not only under a monarchy, but also under a democratic republic the state remains a state, i.e., it retains its fundamental distinguishing feature of transforming the officials, the 'servants of society", its organs, into the masters of society.

"Against this transformation of the state and the organs of the state from servants of society into masters of society—an inevitable transformation in all previous states—the Commune used two infallible means. In the first place, it filled all posts—administrative, judicial, and educational—by election on the basis of universal suffrage of all concerned, subject to recall at any time by the electors. And, in the second place, it paid all officials, high or low, only the wages received by other workers. The highest salary paid by the Commune to anyone was 6,000 francs. In this way a dependable barrier to place-hunting and careerism was set up, even apart from the binding mandates to delegates to representative bodies, which were added besides...."

Engels here approached the interesting boundary line at which consistent democracy, on the one hand, is transformed into socialism and, on the other, demands socialism. For, in order to abolish the state, it is necessary to convert the functions of the civil service into the simple operations of control and accounting that are within the scope and ability of the vast majority of the population, and, subsequently, of every single individual. And if careerism is to be abolished completely, it must be made impossible for "honorable" though profitless posts in the civil service to be used as a springboard to highly lucrative posts in banks or joint-stock companies, as constantly happens in all the freest capitalist countries.

Engels, however, did not make the mistake some Marxists make in dealing, for example, with the question of the right of nations to self-determination, when they argue that is is impossible under capitalism and will be superfluous under socialism. This seemingly clever but actually incorrect statement might be made in regard to any democratic institution, including moderate salaries for officials, because fully consistent democracy is impossible under capitalism, and under socialism all democracy will wither away.

This is a sophism like the old joke about a man becoming bald by losing one more hair.

To develop democracy to the utmost, to find the forms for this development, to test them by practice, and so forth—all this is one of the component tasks of the struggle for the social revolution. Taken separately, no kind of democracy will bring socialism. But in actual life democracy will never be "taken separately"; it will be "taken together" with other things, it will exert its influence on economic life as well, will stimulate its transformation; and in its turn it will be influenced by economic development, and so on. This is the dialectics of living history.

Engels continued:

"... This shattering [Sprengung] of the former state power and its replacement by a new and truly democratic one is described in detail in the third section of *The Civil War*. But it was necessary to touch briefly here once more on some of its features, because in Germany particularly the superstitious belief in the state has passed from philosophy into the general consciousness of the bourgeoisie and even of many workers. According to the philosophical conception, the state is the 'realization of the idea', or the Kingdom of God on earth, translated into philosophical terms, the sphere in which eternal truth and justice are, or should be, realized. And from this follows a superstitious reverence for the state and everything connected with it, which takes root the more readily since people are accustomed from childhood to imagine that the affairs and interests common to the whole of society could not be looked after other than as they have been looked after in the past, that is, through the state and its lucratively positioned officials. And people think they have taken quite an extraordinary bold step forward when they have rid themselves of belief in hereditary monarchy and swear by the democratic republic. In reality, however, the state is nothing but a machine for the oppression of one class by another, and indeed in the democratic republic no less than in the monarchy. And at best it is an evil inherited by the proletariat after its victorious struggle for class supremacy, whose worst sides the victorious proletariat will have to lop off as speedily as possible, just as the Commune had to, until a generation reared in new, free social conditions is able to discard the entire lumber of the state."

Engels warned the Germans not to forget the principles of socialism with regard to the state in general in connection with the substitution of a republic for the monarchy. His warnings now read like a veritable lesson to the Tseretelis and Chernovs, who in their "coalition" practice have revealed a superstitious belief in, and a superstitious reverence for, the state!

Two more remarks. 1. Engels' statement that in a democratic republic, "no less" than in a monarchy, the state remains a "machine for the oppression of one class by another" by no means signifies that the form of oppression makes no difference to the proletariat, as some anarchists "teach". A wider, freer and more open form of the class struggle and of class oppression vastly assists the proletariat in its struggle for the abolition of classes in general.

2. Why will only a new generation be able to discard the entire lumber of the state? This question is bound up with that of overcoming democracy, with which we shall deal now.

ENGELS ON THE OVERCOMING OF DEMOCRACY

Engels came to express his views on this subject when establishing that the term "Social-Democrat" was scientifically wrong.

In a preface to an edition of his articles of the seventies on various subjects, mostly on "international" questions (*Internationales aus dem Volkstaat*), dated January 3, 1894, i.e., written a year and a half before his death, Engels wrote that in all his articles he used the word "Communist", and not "Social-Democrat", because at that time the Proudhonists in France and the Lassalleans[8] in Germany called themselves Social-Democrats.

"... For Marx and myself," continued Engels, "it was therefore absolutely impossible to use such a loose term to characterize our special point of view. Today things are different, and the word ["Social-Democrat"] may perhaps pass muster [mag passieren], inexact [unpassend, unsuitable] though it still is for a party whose economic programme is not merely socialist in general, but downright communist, and whose ultimate political aim is to overcome the whole state and, consequently, democracy as well. The names of real political parties, however, are never wholly appropriate; the party develops while the name stays."[9]

The dialectician Engels remained true to dialectics to the end of his days. Marx and I, he said, had a splendid, scientifically exact name for the party, but there was no real party, i.e., no mass proletarian party. Now (at the end of the 19th century) there was a real party, but its name was scientifically wrong. Never mind, it would "pass muster", so long as the party developed, so long as the scientific inaccuracy of the name was not hidden from it and did not hinder its development on the right direction!

Perhaps some wit would console us Bolsheviks in the manner of Engels: we have a real party, it is developing splendidly; even such a meaningless and ugly term as "Bolshevik" will "pass muster", although it expresses nothing whatever but the purely accidental fact that at the Brussels-London Congress of 1903 we were in the majority. Perhaps now that the persecution of our Party by republicans and "revolutionary" petty-bourgeois democrats in July and August has earned the name "Bolshevik" such universal respect, now that, in addition, this persecution marks the tremendous historical progress our Party has made in its real development—perhaps now even I might hesitate to insist on the suggestion I made in April to change the name of our Party. Perhaps I would propose a "compromise" to my comrades, namely, to call ourselves the Communist Party, but to retain the word "Bolshevik" in brackets.

But the question of the name of the Party is incomparably less important than the question of the attitude of the revolutionary proletariat to the state.

In the usual argument about the state, the mistake is constantly made against which Engels warned and which we have in passing indicated above, namely, it is constantly forgotten that the abolition of the state means also the abolition of democracy; that the withering away of the state means the withering away of democracy.

At first sight this assertion seems exceedingly strange and incomprehensible; indeed, someone may even suspect us of expecting the advent of a system of society in which the principle of subordination of the minority to the majority will not be observed—for democracy means the recognition of this very principle.

No, democracy is not identical with the subordination of the minority to the majority. Democracy is a state which recognizes the subordination of the minority to the majority, i.e., an organization for the systematic use of force by one class against another, by one section of the population against another.

We set ourselves the ultimate aim of abolishing the state, i.e., all organized and systematic violence, all use of violence against people in general. We do not expect the advent of a system of society in which the principle of subordination of the minority to the majority will not be observed. In striving for socialism, however, we are convinced that it will develop into communism and, therefore, that the need for violence against people in general, for the subordination of one man to another, and of one section of the population to another, will vanish altogether since people will become accustomed to observing the elementary conditions of social life without violence and without subordination.

In order to emphasize this element of habit, Engels speaks of a new generation, "reared in new, free social conditions", which will "be able to discard the entire lumber of the state"—of any state, including the democratic-republican state.

In order to explain this, it is necessary to analyze the economic basis of the withering away of the state. □

Chapter 5

The economic basis of the withering away of the state

MARX explains this question most thoroughly in his *Critique of the Gotha Programme* (letter to Bracke, May 5, 1875, which was not published until 1891 when it was printed in *Neue Zeit*, vol. IX, 1, and which has appeared in Russian in a special edition). The polemical part of this remarkable work, which contains a criticism of Lassalleanism, has, so to speak, overshadowed its positive part, namely, the analysis of the connection between the development of communism and the withering away of the state.

1. PRESENTATION OF THE QUESTION BY MARX

From a superficial comparison of Marx's letter to Bracke of May 5, 1875, with Engels' letter to Bebel of March 28, 1875, which we examined above, it might appear that Marx was much more of a "champion of the state" than Engels, and that the difference of opinion between the two writers on the question of the state was very considerable.

Engels suggested to Bebel that all chatter about the state be dropped altogether, that the word "state" be eliminated from the programme altogether and the word "community" substituted for it. Engels even declared that the Commune was no longer a state in the proper sense of the word. Yet Marx even spoke of the "future state in communist society", i.e., he would seem to recognize the need for the state even under communism.

But such a view would be fundamentally wrong. A closer examination shows that Marx's and Engels' views on the state and its withering away were completely identical, and that Marx's expression quoted above refers to the state in the process of withering away.

Clearly, there can be no question of specifying the moment of the future "withering away", the more so since it will obviously be a lengthy process. The apparent difference between Marx and Engels is due to the fact that they dealt with different subjects and pursued different aims. Engels set out to show Bebel graphically, sharply, and in broad outline the utter absurdity of the current prejudices concerning the state (shared to no small degree by Lassalle). Marx only touched upon this question in passing, being interested in another subject, namely, the development of communist society.

The whole theory of Marx is the application of the theory of development—in its most consistent, complete, considered and pithy form—to modern capitalism. Naturally, Marx was faced with the problem of applying this theory both to the forthcoming collapse of capitalism and to the future development of future communism.

On the basis of what facts, then, can the question of the future development of future communism be dealt with?

On the basis of the fact that it has its origin in capitalism, that it develops historically from capitalism, that it is the result of the action of a social force to which capitalism gave birth. There is no trace of an attempt on Marx's part to make up a utopia, to indulge in idle guess-work about what cannot be known. Marx treated the question of communism in the same way as a naturalist would treat the question of the development of, say, a new biological variety, once he knew that it had originated in such and such a way and was changing in such and such a definite direction.

To begin with, Marx brushed aside the confusion the Gotha Programme brought into the question of the relationship between state and society. He wrote:

> "'Present-day society' is capitalist society, which exists in all civilized countries, being more or less free from medieval admixture, more or less modified by the particular historical development of each country, more or less developed. On the other hand, the 'present-day state' changes with a country's frontier. It is different in the Prusso-German Empire from what it is in Switzerland, and different in England from what it is in the United States. 'The present-day state' is, therefore, a fiction.

"Nevertheless, the different states of the different civilized countries, in spite of their motley diversity of form, all have this in common, that they are based on modern bourgeois society, only one more or less capitalistically developed. They have, therefore, also certain essential characteristics in common. In this sense it is possible to speak of the 'present-day state', in contrast with the future, in which its present root, bourgeois society, will have died off.

"The question then arises: what transformation will the state undergo in communist society? In other words, what social functions will remain in existence there that are analogous to present state functions? This question can only be answered scientifically, and one does not get a flea-hop nearer to the problem by a thousandfold combination of the word people with the word state."[1]

After thus ridiculing all talk about a "people's state", Marx formulated the question and gave warning, as it were, that those seeking a scientific answer to it should use only firmly-established scientific data.

The first fact that has been established most accurately by the whole theory of development, by science as a whole—a fact that was ignored by the utopians, and is ignored by the present-day opportunists, who are afraid of the socialist revolution—is that, historically, there must undoubtedly be a special stage, or a special phase, of transition from capitalism to communism.

2. THE TRANSITION FROM CAPITALISM TO COMMUNISM

Marx continued:

"Between capitalist and communist society lies the period of the revolutionary transformation of the one into the other. Corresponding to this is also a political transition period in which the state can be nothing but the revolutionary dictatorship of the proletariat."

Marx bases this conclusion on an analysis of the role played by the proletariat in modern capitalist society, on the data concerning the development of this society, and on the irreconcilability of the antagonistic interests of the proletariat and the bourgeoisie.

Previously the question was put as follows: to achieve its emancipation, the proletariat must overthrow the bourgeoisie, win political power and establish its revolutionary dictatorship.

Now the question is put somewhat differently: the transition from capitalist society—which is developing towards communism—to communist society is impossible without a "political transition period", and the state in this period can only be the revolutionary dictatorship of the proletariat.

What, then, is the relation of this dictatorship to democracy?

We have seen that the *Communist Manifesto* simply places side by side the two concepts: "to raise the proletariat to the position of the ruling class" and "to win the battle of democracy". On the basis of all that has been said above, it is possible to determine more precisely how democracy changes in the transition from capitalism to communism.

In capitalist society, providing it develops under the most favourable conditions, we have a more or less complete democracy in the democratic republic. But this democracy is always hemmed in by the narrow limits set by capitalist exploitation, and consequently always remains, in effect, a democracy for the minority, only for the propertied classes, only for the rich. Freedom in capitalist society always remains about the same as it was in the ancient Greek republics: freedom for the slave-owners. Owing to the conditions of capitalist exploitation, the modern wage slaves are so crushed by want and poverty that "they cannot be bothered with democracy", "cannot be bothered with politics"; in the ordinary, peaceful course of events, the majority of the population is debarred from participation in public and political life.

The correctness of this statement is perhaps most clearly confirmed by Germany, because constitutional legality steadily endured there for a remarkably long time—nearly half a century (1871-1914)—and during this period the Social-Democrats were able to achieve far more than in other countries in the way of "utilizing legality", and organized a larger proportion of the workers into a political party than anywhere else in the world.

What is this largest proportion of politically conscious and active wage slaves that has so far been recorded in capitalist society? One million members of the Social-Democratic Party—out of 15,000,000 wage-workers! Three million organized in trade unions— out of 15,000,000!

Democracy for an insignificant minority, democracy for the rich—that is the democracy of capitalist society. If we look more closely into the machinery of capitalist democracy, we see every-where, in the "petty"—supposedly petty—details of the suffrage (res-idential qualifications, exclusion of women, etc.), in the technique of the representative institutions, in the actual obstacles to the right of assembly (public buildings are not for "paupers"!), in the purely capitalist organization of the daily press, etc., etc.,—we see restric-tion after restriction upon democracy. These restrictions, exceptions, exclusions, obstacles for the poor seem slight, especially in the eyes of one who has never known want himself and has never been in close contact with the oppressed classes in their mass life (and nine out of 10, if not 99 out of 100, bourgeois publicists and politicians come under this category); but in their sum total these restrictions exclude and squeeze out the poor from politics, from active partici-pation in democracy.

Marx grasped this essence of capitalist democracy splendidly when, in analyzing the experience of the Commune, he said that the oppressed are allowed once every few years to decide which particu-lar representatives of the oppressing class shall represent and repress them in parliament!

But from this capitalist democracy—that is inevitably narrow and stealthily pushes aside the poor, and is therefore hypocritical and false through and through—forward development does not proceed simply, directly and smoothly, towards "greater and greater democ-racy", as the liberal professors and petty-bourgeois opportunists would have us believe. No, forward development, i.e., development towards communism, proceeds through the dictatorship of the pro-letariat, and cannot do otherwise, for the resistance of the capitalist exploiters cannot be broken by anyone else or in any other way.

And the dictatorship of the proletariat, i.e., the organization of the vanguard of the oppressed as the ruling class for the purpose of suppressing the oppressors, cannot result merely in an expansion of democracy. Simultaneously with an immense expansion of democracy, which for the first time becomes democracy for the poor, democracy for the people, and not democracy for the money-bags, the dictatorship of the proletariat imposes a series of restrictions on the freedom of the oppressors, the exploiters, the capitalists. We must suppress them in order to free humanity from wage slavery, their resistance must be crushed by force; it is clear that there is no freedom and no democracy where there is suppression and where there is violence.

Engels expressed this splendidly in his letter to Bebel when he said, as the reader will remember, that "the proletariat needs the state, not in the interests of freedom but in order to hold down its adversaries, and as soon as it becomes possible to speak of freedom the state as such ceases to exist".

Democracy for the vast majority of the people, and suppression by force, i.e., exclusion from democracy, of the exploiters and oppressors of the people—this is the change democracy undergoes during the transition from capitalism to communism.

Only in communist society, when the resistance of the capitalists have disappeared, when there are no classes (i.e., when there is no distinction between the members of society as regards their relation to the social means of production), only then "the state... ceases to exist", and "it becomes possible to speak of freedom". Only then will a truly complete democracy become possible and be realized, a democracy without any exceptions whatever. And only then will democracy begin to wither away, owing to the simple fact that, freed from capitalist slavery, from the untold horrors, savagery, absurdities, and infamies of capitalist exploitation, people will gradually become accustomed to observing the elementary rules of social intercourse that have been known for centuries and repeated for thousands of years in all copy-book maxims. They will become accustomed to observing them without force, without coercion, without subordination, without the special apparatus for coercion called the state.

The expression "the state withers away" is very well-chosen, for it indicates both the gradual and the spontaneous nature of the process. Only habit can, and undoubtedly will, have such an effect; for we see around us on millions of occassions how readily people become accustomed to observing the necessary rules of social intercourse when there is no exploitation, when there is nothing that arouses indignation, evokes protest and revolt, and creates the need for suppression.

And so in capitalist society we have a democracy that is curtailed, wretched, false, a democracy only for the rich, for the minority. The dictatorship of the proletariat, the period of transition to communism, will for the first time create democracy for the people, for the majority, along with the necessary suppression of the exploiters, of the minority. Communism alone is capable of providing really complete democracy, and the more complete it is, the sooner it will become unnecessary and wither away of its own accord.

In other words, under capitalism we have the state in the proper sense of the word, that is, a special machine for the suppression of one class by another, and, what is more, of the majority by the minority. Naturally, to be successful, such an undertaking as the systematic suppression of the exploited majority by the exploiting minority calls for the utmost ferocity and savagery in the matter of suppressing, it calls for seas of blood, through which mankind is actually wading its way in slavery, serfdom and wage labor.

Furthermore, during the transition from capitalism to communism suppression is still necessary, but it is now the suppression of the exploiting minority by the exploited majority. A special apparatus, a special machine for suppression, the "state", is still necessary, but this is now a transitional state. It is no longer a state in the proper sense of the word; for the suppression of the minority of exploiters by the majority of the wage slaves of yesterday is comparatively so easy, simple and natural a task that it will entail far less bloodshed than the suppression of the risings of slaves, serfs or wage-laborers, and it will cost mankind far less. And it is compatible with the extension of democracy to such an overwhelming majority of the population that the need for a special machine of suppression will begin to disappear. Naturally, the exploiters are unable to suppress the people without a highly complex machine for performing this task, but the people can suppress the exploiters even with a very simple "machine", almost without a "machine", without a special apparatus, by the simple organization of the armed people (such as the Soviets of Workers' and Soldiers' Deputies, we would remark, running ahead).

Lastly, only communism makes the state absolutely unnecessary, for there is nobody to be suppressed—"nobody" in the sense of a class, of a systematic struggle against a definite section of the population. We are not utopians, and do not in the least deny the possibility and inevitability of excesses on the part of *individual persons*, or the need to stop such excesses. In the first place, however, no special machine, no special apparatus of suppression, is needed for this: this will be done by the armed people themselves, as simply and as readily as any crowd of civilized people, even in modern society, interferes to put a stop to a scuffle or to prevent a woman from being assaulted. And, secondly, we know that the fundamental social cause of excesses, which consist in the violation of the rules of social intercourse, is the exploitation of the people, their want and their poverty. With the removal of this chief cause, excesses will inevitably begin to "wither away". We do not know how quickly and in what succession, but we do know they will wither away. With their withering away the state will also wither away.

Without building utopias, Marx defined more fully what can be defined now regarding this future, namely, the differences between the lower and higher phases (levels, stages) of communist society.

3. THE FIRST PHASE OF COMMUNIST SOCIETY

In the *Critique of the Gotha Programme*, Marx goes into detail to disprove Lassalle's idea that under socialism the worker will receive the "undiminished" or "full product of his labor". Marx shows that from the whole of the social labor of society there must be deducted a reserve fund, a fund for the expansion of production, a fund for the replacement of the "wear and tear" of machinery, and so on. Then, from the means of consumption must be deducted a fund for administrative expenses, for schools, hospitals, old people's homes, and so on.

Instead of Lassalle's hazy, obscure, general phrase ("the full product of his labor to the worker"), Marx makes a sober estimate of exactly how socialist society will have to manage its affairs. Marx proceeds to make a concrete analysis of the conditions of life of a society in which there will be no capitalism, and says:

"What we have to deal with here [in analyzing the programme of the workers' party] is a communist society, not as it has developed on its own foundations, but, on the contrary, just as it emerges from capitalist society; which is thus in every respect, economically, morally, and intellectually, still stamped with the birthmarks of the old society from whose womb it comes."

It is this communist society, which has just emerged into the light of day out of the womb of capitalism and which is in every respect stamped with the birthmarks of the old society, that Marx terms the "first", or lower, phase of communist society.

The means of production are no longer the private property of individuals. The means of production belong to the whole of society. Every member of society, performing a certain part of the socially-necessary work, receives a certificate from society to the effect that he has done a certain amount of work. And with this certificate he receives from the public store of consumer goods a corresponding quantity of products. After a deduction is made of the amount of labor which goes to the public fund, every worker, therefore, receives from society as much as he has given to it.

"Equality" apparently reigns supreme.

But when Lassalle, having in view such a social order (usually called socialism, but termed by Marx the first phase of communism), says that this is "equitable distribution", that this is "the equal right of all to an equal product of labor", Lassalle is mistaken and Marx exposes the mistake.

"Hence, the equal right," says Marx, in this case still certainly conforms to "bourgeois law", which, like all law, implies inequality. All law is an application of an equal measure to different people who in fact are not alike, are not equal to one another. That is why the "equal right" is violation of equality and an injustice. In fact, everyone, having performed as much social labor as another, receives an equal share of the social product (after the above-mentioned deductions).

But people are not alike: one is strong, another is weak; one is married, another is not; one has more children, another has less, and so on. And the conclusion Marx draws is:

"... With an equal performance of labor, and hence an equal share in the social consumption fund, one will in fact receive more than another, one will be richer than another, and so on. To avoid all these defects, the right instead of being equal would have to be unequal."

The first phase of communism, therefore, cannot yet provide justice and equality; differences, and unjust differences, in wealth will still persist, but the exploitation of man by man will have become impossible because it will be impossible to seize the means of production—the factories, machines, land, etc.—and make them private property. In smashing Lassalle's petty-bourgeois, vague phrases about "equality" and "justice" in general, Marx shows the course of development of communist society, which is compelled to abolish at first only the "injustice" of the means of production seized by individuals, and which is unable at once to eliminate the other injustice, which consists in the distribution of consumer goods "according to the amount of labor performed" (and not according to needs).

The vulgar economists, including the bourgeois professors and "our" Tugan, constantly reproach the socialists with forgetting the inequality of people and with "dreaming" of eliminating this inequality. Such a reproach, as we see, only proves the extreme ignorance of the bourgeois ideologists.

Marx not only most scrupulously takes account of the inevitable inequality of men, but he also takes into account the fact that the mere conversion of the means of production into the common property of the whole society (commonly called "socialism") does not remove the defects of distribution and the inequality of "bourgeois laws" which continues to prevail so long as products are divided "according to the amount of labor performed". Continuing, Marx says:

"But these defects are inevitable in the first phase of communist society as it is when it has just emerged, after prolonged birth pangs, from capitalist society. Law can never be higher than the economic structure of society and its cultural development conditioned thereby."

And so, in the first phase of communist society (usually called socialism) "bourgeois law" is not abolished in its entirety, but only in part, only in proportion to the economic revolution so far attained, i.e., only in respect of the means of production. "Bourgeois law" recognizes them as the private property of individuals. Socialism converts them into common property. To that extent—and to that extent alone—"bourgeois law" disappears.

However, it persists as far as its other part is concerned; it persists in the capacity of regulator (determining factor) in the distribution of products and the allotment of labor among the members of society. The socialist principle, "He who does not work shall not eat", is already realized; the other socialist principle, "An equal amount of products for an equal amount of labor", is also already realized. But this is not yet communism, and it does not yet abolish "bourgeois law", which gives unequal individuals, in return for unequal (really unequal) amounts of labor, equal amounts of products.

This is a "defect", says Marx, but it is unavoidable in the first phase of communism; for if we are not to indulge in utopianism, we must not think that having overthrown capitalism people will at once learn to work for society without any rules of law. Besides, the abolition of capitalism does not immediately create the economic prerequisites for such a change.

Now, there are no other rules than those of "bourgeois law". To this extent, therefore, there still remains the need for a state, which, while safeguarding the common ownership of the means of production, would safeguard equality in labor and in the distribution of products.

The state withers away insofar as there are no longer any capitalists, any classes, and, consequently, no class can be suppressed.

But the state has not yet completely withered away, since the still remains the safeguarding of "bourgeois law", which sanctifies actual inequality. For the state to wither away completely, complete communism is necessary.

4. THE HIGHER PHASE OF COMMUNIST SOCIETY

Marx continues:

> "In a higher phase of communist society, after the enslaving subordination of the individual to the division of labor, and with it also the antithesis between mental and physical labor, has vanished, after labor has become not only a livelihood but life's prime want, after the pro-

ductive forces have increased with the all-round development of the individual, and all the springs of co-operative
wealth flow more abundantly—only then can the narrow
horizon of bourgeois law be left behind in its entirety and
society inscribe on its banners: From each according to his
ability, to each according to his needs!"

Only now can we fully appreciate the correctness of Engels'
remarks mercilessly ridiculing the absurdity of combining the words
"freedom" and "state". So long as the state exists there is no freedom.
When there is freedom, there will be no state.

The economic basis for the complete withering away of the
state is such a high state of development of communism at which
the antithesis between mental and physical labor disappears, at
which there consequently disappears one of the principal sources
of modern social inequality—a source, moreover, which cannot on
any account be removed immediately by the mere conversion of the
means of production into public property, by the mere expropriation
of the capitalists.

This expropriation will make it possible for the productive
forces to develop to a tremendous extent. And when we see how
incredibly capitalism is already retarding this development, when we
see how much progress could be achieved on the basis of the level of
technique already attained, we are entitled to say with the fullest confidence that the expropriation of the capitalists will inevitably result in
an enormous development of the productive forces of human society.
But how rapidly this development will proceed, how soon it will reach
the point of breaking away from the division of labor, of doing away
with the antithesis between mental and physical labor, of transforming labor into "life's prime want"—we do not and cannot know.

That is why we are entitled to speak only of the inevitable
withering away of the state, emphasizing the protracted nature of this
process and its dependence upon the rapidity of development of the
higher phase of communism, and leaving the question of the time
required for, or the concrete forms of, the withering away quite open,
because there is no material for answering these questions.

The state will be able to wither away completely when society
adopts the rule: "From each according to his ability, to each accord-

ing to his needs", i.e., when people have become so accustomed to observing the fundamental rules of social intercourse and when their labor has become so productive that they will voluntarily work according to their ability. "The narrow horizon of bourgeois law", which compels one to calculate with the heartlessness of a Shylock whether one has not worked half an hour more than anybody else— this narrow horizon will then be left behind. There will then be no need for society, in distributing the products, to regulate the quantity to be received by each; each will take freely "according to his needs".

From the bourgeois point of view, it is easy to declare that such a social order is "sheer utopia" and to sneer at the socialists for promising everyone the right to receive from society, without any control over the labor of the individual citizen, any quantity of truffles, cars, pianos, etc. Even to this day, most bourgeois "savants" confine themselves to sneering in this way, thereby betraying both their ignorance and their selfish defence of capitalism.

Ignorance—for it has never entered the head of any socialist to "promise" that the higher phase of the development of communism will arrive; as for the greatest socialists' forecast that it will arrive, it presupposes not the present ordinary run of people, who, like the seminary students in Pomyalovsky's stories,[2] are capable of damaging the stocks of public wealth "just for fun", and of demanding the impossible.

Until the "higher" phase of communism arrives, the socialists demand the strictest control by society and by the state over the measure of labor and the measure of consumption; but this control must start with the expropriation of the capitalists, with the establishment of workers' control over the capitalists, and must be exercised not by a state of bureaucrats, but by a state of armed workers.

The selfish defence of capitalism by the bourgeois ideologists (and their hangers-on, like the Tseretelis, Chernovs, and Co.) consists in that they substitute arguing and talk about the distant future for the vital and burning question of present-day politics, namely, the expropriation of the capitalists, the conversion of all citizens into workers and other employees of one huge "syndicate"—the whole state—and the complete subordination of the entire work of this syndicate to a genuinely democratic state, the state of the Soviets of Workers' and Soldiers' Deputies.

In fact, when a learned professor, followed by the philistine, followed in turn by the Tseretelis and Chernovs, talks of wild utopias, of the demagogic promises of the Bolsheviks, of the impossibility of "introducing" socialism, it is the higher stage, or phase, of communism he has in mind, which no one has ever promised or even thought to "introduce", because, generally speaking, it cannot be "introduced".

And this brings us to the question of the scientific distinction between socialism and communism which Engels touched on in his above-quoted argument about the incorrectness of the name "Social-Democrat". Politically, the distinction between the first, or lower, and the higher phase of communism will in time, probably, be tremendous. But it would be ridiculous to recognize this distinction now, under capitalism, and only individual anarchists, perhaps, could invest it with primary importance (if there still are people among the anarchists who have learned nothing from the "Plekhanov" conversion of the Kropotkins, of Grave, Corneliseen, and other "stars" of anarchism into social-chauvinists or "anarcho-trenchists", as Ghe, one of the few anarchists who have still preserved a sense of humor and a conscience, has put it).

But the scientific distinction between socialism and communism is clear. What is usually called socialism was termed by Marx the "first", or lower, phase of communist society. Insofar as the means of production becomes common property, the word "communism" is also applicable here, providing we do not forget that this is not complete communism. The great significance of Marx's explanations is that here, too, he consistently applies materialist dialectics, the theory of development, and regards communism as something which develops out of capitalism. Instead of scholastically invented, "concocted" definitions and fruitless disputes over words (What is socialism? What is communism?), Marx gives an analysis of what might be called the stages of the economic maturity of communism.

In its first phase, or first stage, communism cannot as yet be fully mature economically and entirely free from traditions or vestiges of capitalism. Hence the interesting phenomenon that communism in its first phase retains "the narrow horizon of bourgeois law". Of course, bourgeois law in regard to the distribution of consumer goods inevitably presupposes the existence of the bourgeois state, for law is nothing without an apparatus capable of enforcing the observance of the rules of law.

It follows that under communism there remains for a time not only bourgeois law, but even the bourgeois state, without the bourgeoisie!

This may sound like a paradox or simply a dialectical conundrum of which Marxism is often accused by people who have not taken the slightest trouble to study its extraordinarily profound content.

But in fact, remnants of the old, surviving in the new, confront us in life at every step, both in nature and in society. And Marx did not arbitrarily insert a scrap of "bourgeois" law into communism, but indicated what is economically and politically inevitable in a society emerging out of the womb of capitalism.

Democracy means equality. The great significance of the proletariat's struggle for equality and of equality as a slogan will be clear if we correctly interpret it as meaning the abolition of classes. But democracy means only formal equality. And as soon as equality is achieved for all members of society in relation to ownership of the means of production, that is, equality of labor and wages, humanity will inevitably be confronted with the question of advancing further from formal equality to actual equality, i.e., to the operation of the rule "from each according to his ability, to each according to his needs". By what stages, by means of what practical measures humanity will proceed to this supreme aim we do not and cannot know. But it is important to realize how infinitely mendacious is the ordinary bourgeois conception of socialism as something lifeless, rigid, fixed once and for all, whereas in reality only socialism will be the beginning of a rapid, genuine, truly mass forward movement, embracing first the majority and then the whole of the population, in all spheres of public and private life.

Democracy is of enormous importance to the working class in its struggle against the capitalists for its emancipation. But democracy is by no means a boundary not to be overstepped; it is only one of the stages on the road from feudalism to capitalism, and from capitalism to communism.

Democracy is a form of the state, it represents, on the one hand, the organized, systematic use of force against persons; but, on the other hand, it signifies the formal recognition of equality of citizens, the equal right of all to determine the structure of, and to administer, the state. This, in turn, results in the fact that, at a certain stage in the development of democracy, it first welds together the class that wages a revolutionary struggle against capitalism—the proletariat, and enables it to crush, smash to atoms, wipe off the face of the earth the bourgeois, even the republican-bourgeois, state machine, the standing army, the police and the bureaucracy and to substitute for them a more democratic state machine, but a state machine nevertheless, in the shape of armed workers who proceed to form a militia involving the entire population.

Here "quantity turns into quality": such a degree of democracy implies overstepping the boundaries of bourgeois society and beginning its socialist reorganization. If really all take part in the administration of the state, capitalism cannot retain its hold. The development of capitalism, in turn, creates the preconditions that enable really "all" to take part in the administration of the state. Some of these preconditions are: universal literacy, which has already been achieved in a number of the most advanced capitalist countries, then the "training and disciplining" of millions of workers by the huge, complex, socialized apparatus of the postal service, railways, big factories, large-scale commerce, banking, etc., etc.

Given these economic preconditions, it is quite possible, after the overthrow of the capitalists and the bureaucrats, to proceed immediately, overnight, to replace them in the control over production and distribution, in the work of keeping account of labor and products, by the armed workers, by the whole of the armed population. (The question of control and accounting should not be confused with the question of the scientifically trained staff of engineers, agronomists, and so on. These gentlemen are working today in obedience to the wishes of the capitalists and will work even better tomorrow in obedience to the wishes of the armed workers.)

Accounting and control—that is *mainly* what is needed for the "smooth working", for the proper functioning, of the *first phase* of communist society. *All* citizens are transformed into hired employees of the state, which consists of the armed workers. *All* citizens becomes employees and workers of a *single* countrywide state "syndicate". All that is required is that they should work equally, do their proper share of work, and get equal pay; the accounting and control necessary for this have been *simplified* by capitalism to the utmost and reduced to the extraordinarily simple operations—which any literate person can perform—of supervising and recording, knowledge of the four rules of arithmetic, and issuing appropriate receipts.[1]

When the *majority* of the people begin independently and everywhere to keep such accounts and exercise such control over the capitalists (now converted into employees) and over the intellectual gentry who preserve their capitalist habits, this control will really become universal, general, and popular; and there will be no getting away from it, there will be "nowhere to go".

The whole of society will have become a single office and a single factory, with equality of labor and pay.

But this "factory" discipline, which the proletariat, after defeating the capitalists, after overthrowing the exploiters, will extend to the whole of society, is by no means our ideal, or our ultimate goal. It is only a necessary *step* for thoroughly cleansing society of all the infamies and abominations of capitalist exploitation, *and for further* progress.

From the moment all members of society, or at least the vast majority, have learned to administer the state *themselves*, have taken this work into their own hands, have organized control over the insignificant capitalist minority, over the gentry who wish to preserve their capitalist habits and over the workers who have been thoroughly corrupted by capitalism—from this moment the need for government of any kind begins to disappear altogether. The more complete the democracy, the nearer the moment when it becomes unnecessary. The more democratic the "state" which consists of the armed workers, and which is "no longer a state in the proper sense of the word", the more rapidly *every form* of state begins to wither away.

For when *all* have learned to administer and actually to independently administer social production, independently keep accounts and exercise control over the parasites, the sons of the wealthy, the swindlers and other "guardians of capitalist traditions", the escape from this popular accounting and control will inevitably become so incredibly difficult, such a rare exception, and will probably be accompanied by such swift and severe punishment (for the armed workers are practical men and not sentimental intellectuals, and they scarcely allow anyone to trifle with them), that the *necessity* of observing the simple, fundamental rules of the community will very soon become a *habit*.

Then the door will be thrown wide open for the transition from the first phase of communist society to its higher phase, and with it to the complete withering away of the state. □

Chapter 6

The vulgarisation of Marxism by opportunists

THE question of the relation of the state to the social revolution, and of the social revolution to the state, like the question of revolution generally, was given very little attention by the leading theoreticians and publicists of the Second International (1889-1914). But the most characteristic thing about the process of the gradual growth of opportunism that led to the collapse of the Second International in 1914 is the fact that even when these people were squarely faced with this question they tried to evade it or ignored it.

In general, it may be said that evasiveness over the question of the relation of the proletarian revolution to the state—an evasiveness which benefited and fostered opportunism—resulted in the distortion of Marxism and in its complete vulgarization.

To characterize this lamentable process, if only briefly, we shall take the most prominent theoreticians of Marxism: Plekhanov and Kautsky.

1. PLEKHANOV'S CONTROVERSY WITH THE ANARCHISTS

Plekhanov wrote a special pamphlet on the relation of anarchism to socialism, entitled *Anarchism and Socialism*, which was published in german in 1894.

In treating this subject, Plekhanov contrived completely to evade the most urgent, burning, and most politically essential issue in the struggle against anarchism, namely, the relation of the revolution to the state, and the question of the state in general! His pamphlet falls into two distinct parts: one of them is historical and literary, and contains valuable material on the history of the ideas of Stirner, Proudhon, and others; the other is philistine, and contains a clumsy dissertation on the theme that an anarchist cannot be distinguished from a bandit.

It is a most amusing combination of subjects and most characteristic of Plekhanov's whole activity on the eve of the revolution and during the revolutionary period in Russia. In fact, in the years 1905 to 1917, Plekhanov revealed himself as a semi-doctrinaire and semi-philistine who, in politics, trailed in the wake of the bourgeoisie.

We have now seen how, in their controversy with the anarchists, Marx and Engels with the utmost thoroughness explained their views on the relation of revolution to the state. In 1891, in his foreword to Marx's *Critique of the Gotha Programme*, Engels wrote that "we"—that is, Engels and Marx—"were at that time, hardly two years after the Hague Congress of the [First] International,[1] engaged in the most violent struggle against Bakunin and his anarchists."

The anarchists had tried to claim the Paris Commune as their "own", so to say, as a collaboration of their doctrine; and they completely misunderstood its lessons and Marx's analysis of these lessons. Anarchism has given nothing even approximating true answers to the concrete political questions: Must the old state machine be smashed? And what should be put in its place?

But to speak of "anarchism and socialism" while completely evading the question of the state, and disregarding the whole development of Marxism before and after the Commune, meant inevitably slipping into opportunism. For what opportunism needs most of all is that the two questions just mentioned should not be raised at all. That in itself is a victory for opportunism.

2. KAUTSKY'S CONTROVERSY WITH THE OPPORTUNISTS

Undoubtedly, an immeasurably larger number of Kautsky's works have been translated into Russian than into any other language. It is not without reason that some German Social-Democrats say in jest that Kautsky is read more in Russia than in Germany (let us say, in parenthesis, that this jest has a far deeper historical meaning than those who first made it suspect. The Russian workers, by making in 1905 an unusually great and unprecedented demand for the best works of the best Social-Democratic literature and editions of these works in quantities unheard of in other countries, rapidly transplanted, so to speak, the enormous experience of a neighboring, more advanced country to the young soil of our proletarian movement).

Besides his popularization of Marxism, Kautsky is particularly known in our country for his controversy with the opportunists, with Bernstein at their head. One fact, however, is almost unknown, one which cannot be ignored if we set out to investigate how Kautsky drifted into the morass of unbelievably disgraceful confusion and defence of social-chauvinism during the supreme crisis of 1914-15. This fact is as follows: shortly before he came out against the most prominent representatives of opportunism in France (Millerand and Jaures) and in Germany (Bernstein), Kautsky betrayed very considerable vacillation. The Marxist *Zarya*,[2] which was published in Stuttgart in 1901-02, and advocated revolutionary proletarian views, was forced to enter into controversy with Kautsky and describe as "elastic" the half-hearted, evasive resolution, conciliatory towards the opportunists, that he proposed at the International Socialist Congress in Paris in 1900.[3] Kautsky's letters published in Germany reveal no less hesitancy on his part before he took the field against Bernstein.

Of immeasurably greater significance, however, is the fact that, in his very controversy with the opportunists, in his formulation of the question and his manner of treating it, we can now see, as we study the history of Kautsky's latest betrayal of Marxism, his systematic deviation towards opportunism precisely on the question of the state.

Let us take Kautsky's first important work against opportunism, *Bernstein and the Social-Democratic Programme.* Kautsky refutes Bernstein in detail, but here is a characteristic thing:

Bernstein, in his *Premises of Socialism*, of Herostratean fame, accuses Marxism of "Blanquism" (an accusation since repeated thousands of times by the opportunists and liberal bourgeoisie in Russia against the revolutionary Marxists, the Bolsheviks). In this connection Bernstein dwells particularly on Marx's *The Civil War in France*, and tries, quite unsuccessfully, as we have seen, to identify Marx's views on the lessons of the Commune with those of Proudhon. Bernstein pays particular attention to the conclusion which Marx emphasized in his 1872 preface to the *Communist Manifesto*, namely, that "the working class cannot simply lay hold of the ready-made state machinery and wield it for its own purposes".

This statement "pleased" Bernstein so much that he used it no less than three times in his book, interpreting it in the most distorted, opportunist way.

As we have seen, Marx meant that the working class must smash, break, shatter (*sprengung*, explosion—the expression used by Engels) the whole state machine. But according to Bernstein it would appear as though Marx in these words warned the working class against excessive revolutionary zeal when seizing power.

A cruder more hideous distortion of Marx's idea cannot be imagined.

How, then, did Kautsky proceed in his most detailed refutation of Bernsteinism?

He refrained from analyzing the utter distortion of Marxism by opportunism on this point. He cited the above-quoted passage from Engels' preface to Marx's *Civil War* and said that according to Marx the working class cannot simply take over the ready-made state machinery, but that, generally speaking, it can take it over—and that was all. Kautsky did not say a word about the fact that Bernstein attributed to Marx the very opposite of Marx's real idea, that since 1852 Marx had formulated the task of the proletarian revolution as being to "smash" the state machine.

The result was that the most essential distinction between Marxism and opportunism on the subject of the tasks of the proletarian revolution was slurred over by Kautsky!

"We can quite safely leave the solution of the problems of the proletarian dictatorship of the future," said Kautsky, writing "against" Bernstein. (p.172, German edition)

This is not a polemic against Bernstein, but, in essence, a concession to him, a surrender to opportunism; for at present the opportunists ask nothing better than to "quite safely leave to the future" all fundamental questions of the tasks of the proletarian revolution.

From 1852 to 1891, or for 40 years, Marx and Engels taught the proletariat that it must smash the state machine. Yet, in 1899, Kautsky, confronted with the complete betrayal of Marxism by the opportunists on this point, fraudulently substituted for the question whether it is necessary to smash this machine the question for the concrete forms in which it is to be smashed, and then sough refuge behind the "indisputable" (and barren) philistine truth that concrete forms cannot be known in advance!!

A gulf separates Marx and Kautsky over their attitude towards the proletarian party's task of training the working class for revolution.

Let us take the next, more mature, work by Kautsky, which was also largely devoted to a refutation of opportunist errors. It is his pamphlet, *The Social Revolution*. In this pamphlet, the author chose as his special theme the question of "the proletarian revolution" and "the proletarian regime". He gave much that was exceedingly valuable, but he avoided the question of the state. Throughout the pamphlet the author speaks of the winning of state power—and no more; that is, he has chosen a formula which makes a concession to the opportunists, inasmuch as it admits the possibility of seizing power without destroying the state machine. The very thing which Marx in 1872 declared to be "obsolete" in the programme of the *Communist Manifesto*, is revived by Kautsky in 1902.

A special section in the pamphlet is devoted to the "forms and weapons of the social revolution". Here Kautsky speaks of the mass political strike, of civil war, and of the "instruments of the might of the modern large state, its bureaucracy and the army"; but he does not say a word about what the Commune has already taught the workers. Evidently, it was not without reason that Engels issued a warning, particularly to the German socialists. against "superstitious reverence" for the state.

Kautsky treats the matter as follows: the victorious proletariat "will carry out the democratic programme", and he goes on to formulate its clauses. But he does not say a word about the new material provided in 1871 on the subject of the replacement of bourgeois democracy by proletarian democracy. Kautsky disposes of the question by using such "impressive-sounding" banalities as:

> "Still, it goes without saying that we shall not achieve supremacy under the present conditions. Revolution itself presupposes long and deep-going struggles, which, in themselves, will change our present political and social structure."

Undoubtedly, this "goes without saying," just as the fact that horses eat oats of the Volga flows into the Caspian. Only it is a pity that an empty and bombastic phrase about "deep-going" struggles is used to avoid a question of vital importance to the revolutionary proletariat, namely, what makes its revolution "deep-going" in relation to the state, to democracy, as distinct from previous, non-proletarian revolutions.

By avoiding this question, Kautsky in practice makes a concession to opportunism on this most essential point, although in words he declares stern war against it and stresses the importance of the "idea of revolution" (how much is this "idea" worth when one is afraid to teach the workers the concrete lessons of revolution?), or says, "revolutionary idealism before everything else", or announces that the English workers are now "hardly more than petty bourgeois".

"The most varied form of enterprises—bureaucratic [??], trade unionist, co-operative, private... can exist side by side in socialist society," Kautsky writes. "... There are, for example, enterprises which cannot do without a bureaucratic [??] organization, such as the railways. Here the democratic organization may take the following shape: the workers elect delegates who form a sort of parliament, which establishes the working regulations and supervises the management of the bureaucratic apparatus. The management of other countries may be transferred to the trade unions, and still others may become co-operative enterprises."

This argument is erroneous; it is a step backward compared with the explanations Marx and Engels gave in the seventies, using the lessons of the Commune as an example.

As far as the supposedly necessary "bureaucratic" organization is concerned, there is no difference whatever between a railway and any other enterprise in large-scale machine industry, any factory, large shop, or large-scale capitalist agricultural enterprise. The technique of all these enterprises makes absolutely imperative the strictest discipline, the utmost precision on the part of everyone in carrying out his allotted task, for otherwise the whole enterprise may come to a stop, or machinery or the finished product may be damaged. In all these enterprises the workers will, of course, "elect delegates who will form a sort of parliament".

The whole point, however, is that this "sort of parliament" will not be a parliament in the sense of a bourgeois parliamentary institution. The whole point is that this "sort of parliament" will not merely "establish the working regulations and supervise the management of the bureaucratic apparatus," as Kautsky, whose thinking does not go beyond the bounds of bourgeois parliamentarianism, imagines. In socialist society, the "sort of parliament" consisting of workers' deputies will, of course, "establish the working regulations and supervise the management" of the "apparatus," but this apparatus will not be "bureaucratic."

Kautsky has not reflected at all on Marx's words: "The Commune was a working, not parliamentary, body, executive and legislative at the same time."

Kautsky has not understood at all the difference between bourgeois parliamentarism, which combines democracy (not for the people) with bureaucracy (against the people), and proletarian democracy, which will take immediate steps to cut bureaucracy down to the roots, and which will be able to carry these measures through to the end, to the complete abolition of bureaucracy, to the introduction of complete democracy for the people.

Kautsky here displays the same old "superstitious reverence" for the state, and "superstitious belief" in bureaucracy.

Let us now pass to the last and best of Kautsky's works against the opportunists, his pamphlet *The Road to Power* (which, I believe, has not been published in Russian, for it appeared in 1909, when reaction was at its height in our country). This pamphlet is a big step forward, since it does not deal with the revolutionary programme in general, as the pamphlet of 1899 against Bernstein, or with the tasks of the social revolution irrespective of the time of its occurrence, as the 1902 pamphlet, *The Social Revolution*; it deals with the concrete conditions which compels us to recognize that the "era of revolutions" is setting in.

The author explicitly points to the aggravation of class antagonisms in general and to imperialism, which plays a particularly important part in this respect. After the "revolutionary period of 1789-1871" in Western Europe, he says, a similar period began in the East in 1905. A world war is approaching with menacing rapidity. "It [the proletariat] can no longer talk of premature revolution." "We have entered a revolutionary period." The "revolutionary era is beginning".

These statements are perfectly clear. This pamphlet of Kautsky's should serve as a measure of comparison of what the German Social-Democrats promised to be before the imperialist war and the depth of degradation to which they, including Kautsky himself, sank when the war broke out. "The present situation," Kautsky wrote in the pamphlet under survey, "is fraught with the danger that we [i.e., the German Social-Democrats] may easily appear to be more 'moderate' than we really are." It turned out that in reality the German Social-Democratic Party was much more moderate and opportunist than it appeared to be!

It is all the more characteristic, therefore, that although Kautsky so explicitly declared that the era of revolution had already begun, in the pamphlet which he himself said was devoted to an analysis of the "political revolution", he again completely avoided the question of the state.

These evasions of the question, these omissions and equivocations, inevitably added up to that complete swing-over to opportunism with which we shall now have to deal.

Kautsky, the German Social-Democrats' spokesman, seems to have declared: I abide by revolutionary views (1899), I recognize, above all, the inevitability of the social revolution of the proletariat (1902), I recognize the advent of a new era of revolutions (1909). Still, I am going back on what Marx said as early as 1852, since the question of the tasks of the proletarian revolution in relation to the state is being raised (1912).

It was in this point-blank form that the question was put in Kautsky's controversy with Pannekoek.

3. KAUTSKY'S CONTROVERSY WITH PANNEKOEK

In opposing Kautsky, Pannekoek came out as one of the representatives of the "Left radical" trend which included Rosa Luxemburg, Karl Radek, and others. Advocating revolutionary tactics, they were united in the conviction that Kautsky was going over to the "Centre", which wavered in an unprincipled manner between

Marxism and opportunism. This view was proved perfectly correct by the war, when this "Centrist" (wrongly called Marxist) trend, or Kautskyism, revealed itself in all its repulsive wretchedness.

In an article touching on the question of the state, entitled "Mass Action and Revolution" (*Neue Zeit*, 1912, Vol.XXX, 2), Pannekoek described Kautsky' s attitude as one of "passive radicalism", as "a theory of inactive expectancy". "Kautsky refuses to see the process of revolution," wrote Pannekoek (p.616). In presenting the matter in this way, Pannekoek approached the subject which interests us, namely, the tasks of the proletarian revolution in relation to the state.

> "The struggle of the proletariat," he wrote, "is not merely a struggle against the bourgeoisie for state power, but a struggle *against* state power.... The content of this [the proletarian] revolution is the destruction and dissolution [Auflosung] of the instruments of power of the state with the aid of the instruments of power of the proletariat. (p.544) "The struggle will cease only when, as the result of it, the state organization is completely destroyed. The organization of the majority will then have demonstrated its superiority by destroying the organization of the ruling minority." (p.548)

The formulation in which Pannekoek presented his ideas suffers from serious defects. But its meaning is clear nonetheless, and it is interesting to note how Kautsky combated it.

> "Up to now," he wrote, "the antithesis between the Social-Democrats and the anarchists has been that the former wished to win the state power while the latter wished to destroy it. Pannekoek wants to do both." (p.724)

Although Pannekoek's exposition lacks precision and concreteness—not to speak of other shortcomings of his article which have no bearing on the present subject—Kautsky seized precisely on the point of principle raised by Pannekoek; and on this fundamental point of principle Kautsky completely abandoned the Marxist position and went over wholly to opportunism. His definition of the distinction between the Social-Democrats and the anarchists is absolutely wrong; he completely vulgarizes and distorts Marxism.

The distinction between Marxists and the anarchists is this: (1) The former, while aiming at the complete abolition of the state, recognize that this aim can only be achieved after classes have been abolished by the socialist revolution, as the result of the establishment of socialism, which leads to the withering away of the state. The latter want to abolish he state completely overnight, not understanding the conditions under which the state can be abolished. (2) The former recognize that after the proletariat has won political power it must completely destroy the old state machine and replace it by a new one consisting of an organization of the armed workers, after the type of the Commune. The latter, while insisting on the destruction of the state machine, have a very vague idea of what the proletariat will put in its place and how it will use its revolutionary power. The anarchists even deny that the revolutionary proletariat should use the state power, they reject its revolutionary dictatorship. (3) The former demand that the proletariat be trained for revolution by utilizing the present state. The anarchists reject this.

In this controversy, it is not Kautsky but Pannekoek who represents Marxism, for it was Marx who taught that the proletariat cannot simply win state power in the sense that the old state apparatus passes into new hands, but must smash this apparatus, must break it and replace it by a new one.

Kautsky abandons Marxism for the opportunist camp, for this destruction of the state machine, which is utterly unacceptable to the opportunists, completely disappears from his argument, and he leaves a loophole for them in that "conquest" may be interpreted as the simple acquisition of a majority.

To cover up his distortion of Marxism, Kautsky behaves like a doctrinaire: he puts forward a "quotation" from Marx himself. In 1850, Marx wrote that a "resolute centralization of power in the hands of the state authority" was necessary, and Kautsky triumphantly asks: does Pannekoek want to destroy "Centralism"?

This is simply a trick, like Bernstein's identification of the views of Marxism and Proudhonism on the subject of federalism as against centralism.

Kautsky's "quotation" is neither here nor there. Centralism is possible with both the old and the new state machine. If the workers voluntarily unite their armed forces, this will be centralism, but it will be based on the "complete destruction" of the centralized state apparatus—the standing army, the police, and the bureaucracy. Kautsky acts like an outright swindler by evading the perfectly well-known arguments of Marx and Engels on the Commune and plucking out a quotation which has nothing to do with the point at issue.

> "Perhaps he [Pannekoek]," Kautsky continues, "wants to abolish the state functions of the officials? But we cannot do without officials even in the party and trade unions, let alone in the state administration. And our programme does not demand the abolition of state officials, but that they be elected by the people.... We are discussing here not the form the administrative apparatus of the ' future state' will assume, but whether our political struggle abolishes [literally dissolves - auflost] the state power *before we have captured it.* [Kautsky's italics] Which ministry with its officials could be abolished?" Then follows an enumeration of the ministeries of education, justice, finance, and war. "No, not one of the present ministries will be removed by our political struggle against the government.... I repeat, in order to prevent misunderstanding: we are not discussing here the form the 'future state' will be given by the victorious Social- Democrats, but how the present state is changed by our opposition." (p.725)

This is an obvious trick. Pannekoek raised the question of revolution. Both the title of his article and the passages quoted above clearly indicate this. By skipping to the question of "opposition", Kautksy substitutes the opportunist for the revolutionary point of view. What he says means: at present we are an opposition; what we shall be after we have captured power, that we shall see. Revolution has vanished! And that is exactly what the opportunists wanted.

The point at issue is neither opposition nor political struggle in general, but revolution. Revolution consists in the proletariat destroying the "administrative apparatus" and the whole state machine, replacing it by a new one, made up of the armed workers. Kautsky displays a "superstitious reverence" for "ministries"; but why can they not be replaced, say, by committees of specialists working under sovereign, all-powerful Soviets of Workers' and Soldiers' Deputies?

The point is not at all whether the "ministries" will remain, or whether "committees of specialists" or some other bodies will be set up; that is quite immaterial. The point is whether the old state machine (bound by thousands of threads to the bourgeoisie and permeated through and through with routine and inertia) shall remain, or be destroyed and replaced by a new one. Revolution consists not in the new class commanding, governing with the aid of the old state machine, but in this class smashing this machine and commanding, governing with the aid of a new machine. Kautsky slurs over this basic idea of Marxism, or he does not understand it at all.

His question about officials clearly shows that he does not understand the lessons of the Commune or the teachings of Marx. "We cannot to without officials even in the party and the trade unions...."

We cannot do without officials under capitalism, under the rule of the bourgeoisie. The proletariat is oppressed, the working people are enslaved by capitalism. Under capitalism, democracy is restricted, cramped, curtailed, mutilated by all the conditions of wage slavery, and the poverty and misery of the people. This and this alone is the reason why the functionaries of our political organizations and trade unions are corrupted—or rather tend to be corrupted—by the conditions of capitalism and betray a tendency to become bureaucrats, i.e., privileged persons divorced from the people and standing above the people.

That is the essence of bureaucracy; and until the capitalists have been expropriated and the bourgeoisie overthrown, even proletarian functionaries will inevitably be "bureaucratized" to a certain extent.

According to Kautsky, since elected functionaries will remain under socialism, so will officials, so will the bureaucracy! This is exactly where he is wrong. Marx, referring to the example of the Commune, showed that under socialism functionaries will cease to be "bureaucrats", to be "officials", they will cease to be so in proportion as—in addition to the principle of election of officials—the principle of recall at any time is also introduced, as salaries are reduced to the level of the wages of the average workman, and as parliamentary institutions are replaced by "working bodies, executive and legislative at the same time".

As a matter of fact, the whole of Kautsky's argument against Pannekoek, and particularly the former's wonderful point that we cannot do without officials even in our party and trade union organizations, is merely a repetition of Bernstein's old "arguments" against Marxism in general. In his renegade book, *The Premises of Socialism*, Bernstein combats the ideas of "primitive" democracy, combats what he calls "doctrinaire democracy": binding mandates, unpaid officials, impotent central representative bodies, etc. to prove that this "primitive" democracy is unsound, Bernstein refers to the experience of the British trade unions, as interpreted by the Webbs.[4] Seventy years of development "in absolute freedom", he says (p.137, German edition), convinced the trade unions that primitive democracy was useless, and they replaced it by ordinary democracy, i.e., parliamentarism combined with bureaucracy.

In reality, the trade unions did not develop "in absolute freedom" but in absolute capitalist slavery, under which, it goes without saying, a number of concessions to the prevailing evil, violence, falsehood, exclusion of the poor from the affairs of "higher" administration, "cannot be done without". Under socialism much of "primitive" democracy will inevitably be revived, since, for the first time in the history of civilized society the mass of the population will rise to taking an independent part, not only in voting and elections, but also in the everyday administration of the state. Under socialism all will govern in turn and will soon become accustomed to no one governing.

Marx's critico-analytical genius saw in the practical measures of the Commune the turning-point which the opportunists fear and do not want to recognize because of their cowardice, because they do not want to break irrevocably with the bourgeoisie, and which the anarchists do not want to see, either because they are in a hurry or because they do not understand at all the conditions of great social changes. "We must not even think of destroying the old state machine; how can we do without ministries and officials" argues the opportunist, who is completely saturated with philistinism and who, at bottom, not only does not believe in revolution, in the creative power of revolution, but lives in mortal dread of it (like our Mensheviks and Socialist-Revolutionaries).

"We must think only of destroying the old state machine; it is no use probing into the concrete lessons of earlier proletarian revolutions and analyzing what to put in the place of what has been destroyed, and how," argues the anarchist (the best of the anarchist, of course, and not those who, following the Kropotkins and Co., trail behind the bourgeoisie). Consequently, the tactics of the anarchist become the tactics of despair instead of a ruthlessly bold revolutionary effort to solve concrete problems while taking into account the practical conditions of the mass movement.

Marx teaches us to avoid both errors; he teaches us to act with supreme boldness in destroying the entire old state machine, and at the same time he teaches us to put the question concretely: the Commune was able in the space of a few weeks to start building a new, proletarian state machine by introducing such-and-such measures to provide wider democracy and to uproot bureaucracy. Let us learn revolutionary boldness from the Communards; let us see in their practical measures the outline of really urgent and immediately possible measures, and then, following this road, we shall achieve the complete destruction of bureaucracy.

The possibility of this destruction is guaranteed by the fact that socialism will shorten the working day, will raise the people to a new life, will create such conditions for the majority of the population as will enable everybody, without exception, to perform "state functions", and this will lead to the complete withering away of every form of state in general.

> "Its object [the object of the mass strike]," Kautsky continues, "cannot be to destroy the state power; its only object can be to make the government compliant on some specific question, or to replace a government hostile to the proletariat by one willing to meet it half-way [*entgegenkommende*]... But never, under no circumstances can it [that is, the proletarian victory over a hostile government] lead to the destruction of the state power; it can lead only to a certain shifting [*verschiebung*] of the balance of forces within the state power.... The aim of our political struggle remains, as in the past, the conquest of state power by winning a majority in par-

liament and by raising parliament to the ranks of master
of the government." (pp.726, 727, 732)

This is nothing but the purest and most vulgar opportunism: repudiating revolution in deeds, while accepting it in words.
Kautsky's thoughts go no further than a "government... willing to
meet the proletariat half-way"—a step backward to philistinism compared with 1847, when the *Communist Manifesto* proclaimed "the
organization of the proletariat as the ruling class".

Kautsky will have to achieve his beloved "unity" with the
Scheidmanns, Plekhanovs, and Vanderveldes, all of whom agree to
fight for a government "willing to meet the proletariat half-way".

We, however, shall break with these traitors to socialism, and
we shall fight for the complete destruction of the old state machine,
in order that the armed proletariat itself *may become the government.*
These are two vastly different things.

Kautsky will have to enjoy the pleasant company of the Legiens
and Davids, Plekhanovs, Potresovs, Tseretelis, and Chernovs, who are
quite willing to work for the "shifting of the balance of forces within
the state power", for "winning a majority in parliament", and "raising
parliament to the ranks of master of the government". A most worthy
object, which is wholly acceptable to the opportunists and which
keeps everything within the bounds of the bourgeois parliamentary
republic.

We, however, shall break with the opportunists; and the entire
class-conscious proletariat will be with us in the fight—not to "shift
the balance of forces", but to overthrow the bourgeoisie, to destroy
bourgeois parliamentarism, for a democratic republic after the type
of the Commune, or a republic of Soviets of Workers' and Soldiers'
Deputies, for the revolutionary dictatorship of the proletariat.

To the right of Kautsky in international socialism there are
trends such as *Socialist Monthly*[5] in Germany (Legien, David, Kolb,
and many others, including the Scandinavian Stauning and Branting),
Jaures' followers and Vandervelde in France and Belgium; Turait,
Treves, and other Right-wingers of the Italian Party; the Fabians and
"Independents" (the Independent labor Party, which, in fact, has

always been dependent on the Liberals) in Britain; and the like. All these gentry, who play a tremendous, very often a predominant role in the parliamentary work and the press of their parties, repudiate outright the dictatorship of the proletariat and pursue a policy of undisguised opportunism. In the eyes of these gentry, the "dictatorship" of the proletariat "contradicts" democracy!! There is really no essential distinction between them and the petty-bourgeois democrats.

Taking this circumstance into consideration, we are justified in drawing the conclusion that the Second International, that is, the overwhelming majority of its official representatives, has completely sunk into opportunism. The experience of the Commune has been not only ignored but distorted. far from inculcating in the workers' minds the idea that the time is nearing when they must act to smash the old state machine, replace it by a new one, and in this way make their political rule the foundation for the socialist reorganization of society, they have actually preached to the masses the very opposite and have depicted the "conquest of power" in a way that has left thousands of loopholes for opportunism.

The distortion and hushing up of the question of the relation of the proletarian revolution to the state could not but play an immense role at a time when states, which possess a military apparatus expanded as a consequence of imperialist rivalry, have become military monsters which are exterminating millions of people in order to settle the issue as to whether Britain or Germany—this or that finance capital—is to rule the world. □

Endnotes

Chapter 1: Class society and the state

[1] See Frederick Engels, The Origin of the Family, Private Property and the State (Karl Marx and Frederick Engels, Selected Works, Vol. 3, Moscow, 1973, pp. 326-27).

Further below, on pp. 393-95, 395-99 of the volume, Lenin is quoting from the same work by Engels (op. cit., pp. 327-30).

[2] Gentile, or tribal, organisation of society—the primitive communal system, or the first socio-economic formation in history. The tribal commune was a community of blood relatives linked by economic and social ties. The tribal system went through the matriarchal and the patriarchal periods. The patriarchate culminated in primitive society becoming a class society and in the rise of the state. Relations of production under the primitive communal system were based on social ownership of the means of production and equalitarian distribution of all products. This corresponded in the main to the low level of the productive forces and to their character at the time.

For the primitive communal system, see Karl Marx, Conspectus of Lewis Morgan's "Ancient Society", and Frederick Engels. The Origin of the Family, Private Property and the State (Karl Marx and Frederick Engels, Selected Works, Vol. 3, Moscow, 1973, pp. 204-334).

[3] See Frederick Engels, Anti-Duhring, Moscow, 1969, pp. 332-33. Further down, on p. 404 of this volume, Lenin is quoting from the same work by Engels (op. cit., p. 220).

[4] Thirty Years' War (1618-48), the first European war, resulted from an aggravation of the antagonisms between various alignments of European states, and took the form of a struggle

between Protestants and Catholics. It began with a revolt in Bohemia against the tyranny of the Hapsburg monarchy and the onslaught of Catholic reaction. The states which then entered the war formed two camps. The Pope, the Spanish and Austrian Hapsburgs and the Catholic princes of Germany, who rallied to the Catholic Church, opposed the Protestant countries— Bohemia, Denmark, Sweden, the Dutch Republic, and a number of German states that had accepted the Reformation. The Protestant countries were backed by the French kings, enemies of the Hapsburgs. Germany became the chief battlefield and object of military plunder and predatory claims. The war ended in 1648 with the signing of the Peace Treaty of Westphalia, which completed the political dismemberment of Germany.

[5] See Karl Marx, The Poverty of Philosophy, Moscow, 1973, pp. 151-52.

[6] See Karl Marx and Frederick Engels, Selected Works, Vol. 1, Moscow, 1973, p. 137.

[7] Gotha Programme—the programme adopted by the Socialist Workers' Party of Germany in 1875, at the Gotha Congress, which united two German socialist parties, namely, the Eisenachers-led by August Bebel and Wilhelm Liebknecht and influenced by Marx and Engcls-and the Lassalleans. The programme betrayed eclecticism and was opportunist, because the Eisenachers had made concessions to the Lassalleans on major issues and accepted Lassallean formulations. Marx in his Critique of the Gotha Programme, and Engels in his letter to Bebel of March 18-28, 11475, devastated the Gotha Programme, which they regarded as a serious step backwards compared with the Eisenach programme of 1869.

Chapter 2: The experience of 1848-51

[1] See Karl Marx, The Poverty of Philosophy, Moscow, 1973, P. 151.

[2] See Karl Marx and Frederick Engels, Selected Works, Vol. 1, Moscow, 1973, pp. 118-19 and 126.

[3] See Karl Marx, The Eighteenth Brumaire of Louis Bonaparte (Karl Marx and Frederick Engels, Selected Works, Vol. I, Moscow, 1973, p. 477).

Further below, on pp. 414-15 of this volume, Lenin is quoting from Engels's preface to the third edition of the work (op. cit., p. 396).

[4] Die Neue Zeit (New Times)—theoretical journal of the German Social-Democratic Party, published in Stuttgart from 1883 to 1923. It was edited by Karl Kautsky till October 1917 and by Heinrich Cunow in the subsequent period. It published some of Marx's and Engels's writings for the first time. Engels offered advice to its editors and often criticised them for departures from Marxism.

In the second half of the nineties, upon Engels's death, the journal began systematically to publish revisionist articles, including a serial by Bernstein entitled "Problems of Socialism". which initiated a revisionist campaign against Marxism. During the First World War the journal adhered to a Centrist position, and virtually hacked the social-chauvinists.

[5] See Karl Marx and Frederick Engels, Selected Correspondence, Moscow, 1965, p. tb').

Chapter 3: The experience of the Paris Commune. Marx's analysis

[1] See Karl Marx and Frederick Engels, Selected Works, Vol. 1, Moscow, 1962, p. 22.

[2] See Karl Marx and Frederick Engels, Selected Correspondence. Moscow, 1965, pp. 262-63.

[3] See Karl Marx, The Civil War in France (Karl Marx and Frederick Engels, Selected Works, Vol. 2, Moscow, 1973, pp. 217-21).

Further below, on pp. 426, 427, 432-436 of this volume, Lenin is quoting from the same work by Marx (op. cit., pp. 222, 220-23).

[4] The Girondists—a political grouping during the French bourgeois revolution of the late eighteenth century, expressed the interests of the moderate bourgeoisie. They wavered between revolution and counter-revolution, and made deals with the monarchy.

Chapter 4: Supplementary explanations by Engels

[1] See Frederick Engels, The Housing Question (Karl Marx and Frederick Engels, Selected Works, Vol. 2, Moscow, 1973, pp. 317-18).

Further below, on pp. 439-40 of this volume, Lenin is quoting from the same work by Engels (op. cit., pp. 370, 355).

[2] Lenin is referring to the articles "L'indifferenza in materia polit-
ica" by Karl Marx and "Dell' Autorita" by Frederick Engels
(Almanacco Republicano per l'anno 1874). Further below, on
pp. 440-41, 442, 442-43 of this volume, Lenin is quoting from
the same articles.

[3] See Karl Marx and Frederick Engels, Selected Correspondence,
Moscow, 1965, pp. 293-94.

[4] Erfurt Programme—the programme adopted by the German
Social-Democratic Party at its Erfurt Congress in October 1891.
A step forward compared with the Gotha Programme (1875), it
was based on Marx's doctrine of the inevitable downfall of the
capitalist mode of production and its replacement by the socialist mode. It stressed the necessity for the working class to wage
a political struggle, pointed out the party's role as the leader
of that struggle, and so on. But it also made serious concessions to opportunism. Engels criticised the original draft of the
programme in detail in his work A Critique of the Draft Social-
Democratic Programme of 1891 It was virtually a critique of the
opportunism of the Second International as a whole. But the
German Social-Democratic leaders concealed Engels's critique
from the rank and file, and disregarded his highly important
comments in drawing up the final text of the programme. Lenin
considered the fact that the Erfurt Programme said nothing
about the dictatorship of the proletariat to be its chief defect and
a cowardly concession to opportunism.

[5] The Anti-Socialist Law (Exceptional Law Against the Socialists)
was enacted in Germany by the Bismarck government in 1878
to combat the working-class and socialist movement. Under this
law, all Social-Democratic Party organisations, all mass organisations of the workers, and the working-class press were banned,
socialist literature was confiscated and the Social-Democrats
were persecuted, to the point of banishment. These repressive measures did not, however, break the Social-Democratic
Party, which readjusted itself to illegal conditions. Der Sozial-
Demokrat, the party's Central Organ, was published abroad and
party congresses were held at regular intervals (1880, 1883 and
1887). In Germany herself, the Social-Democratic organisations
and groups were coming back to life underground, an illegal

Central Committee leading their activities. Besides, the Party widely used legal opportunities to establish closer links with the working people, and its influence was growing steadily. At the Reichstag elections in 1890, it polled three times as many votes as in 1878. Marx and Engels did much to help the Social-Democrats. In 1890 popular pressure and the growing working-class movement led to the annulment of the Anti-Socialist Law.

[6] See Karl Marx and Frederick Engels, Selected Works, Vol. 2, Moscow, 1973, pp. 178-89.

Further below, on pp. 454, 455, 456-58 of this volume, Lenin is quoting from the same work (op. cit., pp. 179-80, 184, 187-89).

[7] The Los-von-Kirche-Bewegung (the "Leave-the-Church" movement), or Kirchenaustrittsbewegung (Movement to Secede from the Church) assumed a vast scale in Germany before the First World War. In January 1914 Neue Zeit began, with the revisionist Paul Gdhre's article "Kirchenaustrittsbewegung und Sozialdemokratie" ("The Movement to Secede from the Church and Social-Democracy"), to discuss the attitude of the German Social-Democratic Party to the movement. During that discussion prominent German Social-Democratic leaders failed to rebuff Göhre, who affirmed that the party should remain neutral towards the Movement to Secede from the Church and forbid its members to engage in propaganda against religion and the Church on behalf of the party.

Lenin took notice of the discussion while working on material for Imperialism, the Highest Stage of Capitalism (see present edition, Vol. 39, p. 591).

[8] Lassalleans—supporters of the German petty-bourgeois socialist Ferdinand Lassalle, members of the General Association of German Workers founded at the Congress of Workers' Organisations, held in Leipzig in 1863, to counterbalance the bourgeois progressists who were trying to gain influence over the working class. The first President of the Association was Lassalle, who formulated its programme and the fundamentals of its tactics. The Association's political programme was declared to be the struggle for universal suffrage, and its economic programme, the struggle for workers' production associ-

ations, to be subsidised by the state. In their practical activities, Lassalle and his followers adapted themselves to the hegemony of Prussia and supported the Great Power policy of Bismarck. "Objectively," wrote Engels to Marx on January 27, 1865, "this was a base action and a betrayal of the whole working-class movement to the Prussians." Marx and Engels frequently and sharply criticised the theory, tactics, and organisational principles of the Lassalleans as an opportunist trend in the German working-class movement.

[9] See Frederick Engels, "Vorwort zur Broschüre Internationales aus dem 'Volksstaat' (1871-1875)", Marx-Engels, Werke, Bd. 22, Berlin, 1963, S. 417-18.

Chapter 5: The economic basis of the withering away of the state

[1] See Karl Marx, Critique of the Gotha Programme (Karl Marx and Frederick Engels, Selected Works, Vol. 3, Moscow, 1973, p. 26). Further below, on pp. 464, 470, 471-73 of this volume, Lenin is quoting from the same work by Marx (op. cit., pp. 26, 17, 19).

[2] Reference is to the pupils of a seminary who won notoriety by their extreme ignorance and barbarous customs. They were portrayed by N. G. Pomyalovsky, a Russian author.

Chapter 6: The vulgarisation of Marxism by opportunists

[*] The MS. continues as follows:

Chapter VII: The Experience of the Russian Revolutions of 1905 and 1917

The subject indicated in the title of this chapter is so vast that volumes could be written about it. In the present pamphlet we shall have to confine ourselves, naturally, to the most important lessons provided by experience, those bearing directly upon the tasks of the proletariat in the revolution with regard to state power. [Here the manuscript breaks off—Ed.]

[1] The Hague Congress of the First international sat from September 2-7, 1872. It was attended by 65 delegates, among whom were Marx and Engels. The powers of the General Council and the political activity of the proletariat were among the items on the agenda. The Congress deliberations were marked throughout by a sharp struggle against the Bakuninists.

The Congress passed a resolution extending the General Council's powers. Its resolution "On the Political Activity of the Proletariat" stated that the proletariat should organise a political party of its own to ensure the triumph of the social revolution and that the winning of political power was becoming its great task. The Congress expelled Bakunin and Guillaume from the International as disorganisers and founders of a new, anti-proletarian party.

[2] Zarya (Dawn)—a Marxist scientific and political journal published in Stuttgart in 1901-02 by the editors of Iskra. Four issues appeared in three instalments.

[3] Reference is to the Fifth World Congress of the Second international, which met in Paris from September 23 to 27, 1900. On the fundamental issue, "The Winning of Political Power, and Alliances with Bourgeois Parties", whose discussion was prompted by A. Millerand becoming a member of the Valdeck-Rousseau counter-revolutionary government, the Congress carried a motion tabled by Kautsky. The resolution said that "the entry of a single Socialist into a bourgeois Ministry cannot be considered as the normal beginning for winning political power: it can never be anything but a temporary and exceptional makeshift in an emergency situation". Afterwards opportunists frequently referred to this point to justify their collaboration with the bourgeoisie.

Zarya published (No. 1, April 1901) an article by Plekhanov entitled "A Few Words About the Latest World Socialist Congress in Paris. An Open Letter to the Comrades Who Have Empowered Me", which sharply criticised Kautsky' s resolution.

[4] This refers to Sydney and Beatrice Webb, Industrial Democracy.

[5] Socialist Monthly (Sozialistische Monatshefte)—the principal journal of the opportunists among the German Social-Democrats, a periodical of international opportunism. It was published in Berlin from 1897 to 1933. During the world imperialist war of 1914-18 it took a social-chauvinist stand.

Liberation News.org
Website of the Party for Socialism and Liberation

Featuring

- **News**
- **Analysis**
- **Militant Journalism**
- **Video and Podcasts**
- **Downloadable Posters and Art**
- **Event Listings and more!**